REMEMBER SENGHENNYDD

Remember Senghenydd:

the colliery disaster of 1913

Editor: Jen Llywelyn

First published in 2013

© Jen Llywelyn (ed.)

© Myrddin ap Dafydd/Gwasg Carreg Gwalch 2013

ISBN: 978-1-84524-208-4

Cover design. Eleri Owen

Cover photograph: the Universal Colliery, 14 October 1913
(W. Benton, 1913)

Published by Gwasg Carreg Gwalch,
12 Iard yr Orsaf, Llanrwst, Wales, LL26 0EH
tel: 01492 624031
fax: 01492 641502
email: llyfrau@carreg-gwalch.com
internet: www.carreg-gwalch.com

Dedication

To all coal-miners, past and present,
and their families

Senghenydd, 2013

Contents

Introduction

Senghenydd is a small village in south Wales, near Caerffili. In 1891, before the Universal Pit was first sunk, the population was around 100. But after the sinking of the York and the Lancaster shafts the population began to increase, quite quickly. By 1911 it numbered 5,895.

As the pit increased in size during the Anglo-Boer War, some of the 'districts' underground were named after South African settlements where British garrisons had been relieved: Pretoria, Mafeking, Kimberley, Ladysmith. Many who went to work in the pit had served in that war.

Wales had been suffering downturns in industry for several years, except in coal-mining, especially in the south-west of the country. The slate industry in Gwynedd had declined, following a boom-time while Liverpool and Manchester had needed Welsh slates for roofing their houses and factories. The lead and silver mines in Ceredigion were running low. Poverty in rural areas was rife. And there was always the threat of another war – in which coal-miners, as producers of coal for shipping and industry, would not be required to fight. Men needed to earn money for their families. Pit work had a certain appeal.

The coal-owners at Senghenydd called for workers; they offered a higher wage per shift than other pits. Men (and their families) came from far and wide to take advantage of this higher income – not just from all over Wales, but from England and Ireland too.

But a long career in coal-mining was never guaranteed ...

The situation in America seems to have been different from that in Wales. During the nineteenth century, the Reverend W. D. Evans wrote regular letters from America to the Welsh-language publication *Baner ac Amserau Cymru*. On 30 March 1881 the following paragraph appeared (translated from the Welsh by W. D. Evans' great-niece Margaret Morgan Jones):

The coalmining areas of Southern Pennsylvania are the largest and most prosperous in the country. Anthracite is the coal mined here and it is abundant in the counties of Carbon, Lackawanna, Luzerne, Schuylkill, Columbia, Northumberland and Dauphin with thousands of Welsh people living in these regions. People who are familiar with coalmining, in Wales as well as America, say that the methods used in America are more advanced than those in Wales. Every mine-proprietor in America is legally obliged to safeguard that enough air is circulating within the pits to make the Davy lamps surplus to requirements, apart from special or unforeseen circumstances. The injected air is diverted into eight or ten different channels and it is quantified on a weekly basis. It is said that in the Pen-y-graig mine in south Wales, where a major accident took place recently, 70,000 cubic feet of air was circulating at the time of the disaster and this was considered to be acceptable. In this part of America, an average of 85,000 cubic feet of air per minute circulates for the benefit of less manpower than that in Wales, with the result that an accident is a rare occurrence here. Another contributory factor must be the hours worked by miners in America; they only work during daytime, whereas in Wales, it is a 24-hour shift system.

Rev. W. D. Evans, From Aberystwyth to San Francisco: the Welsh community in America in the later nineteenth century (*trans. Margaret Morgan Jones, publ. Gwasg Carreg Gwalch, 2013*)

At the time of the second Senghenydd disaster there were 950 men working underground. About half of this day shift were working on the west side of the mine. By 8 o'clock they had all been lowered down the mine. At ten past eight there was a terrific explosion, the noise of screaming tearing metal, and the crash of falling timber. 439 men were killed.

For the next few months – well into 1914 – the disaster ruled the lives of local miners. They worked tirelessly to retrieve the bodies of their comrades, many of whom were never found. William John, aged thirty-one, died under a roof fall while involved in the rescue operation.

The mine was not used for production again. It was finally stopped with rubble and concrete in 1979.

Miners are still working under dangerous conditions throughout the world. In 2010 the copper mine in Copiapó, Chili, was world news when thirty-three miners were trapped below ground, due to the negligence of the mine management. Nearer to home, in 2011 four miners died in the Gleision Colliery in south Wales. The pit manager was later charged with 'gross negligence manslaughter'.

Officially, however, Gleision does not count as a 'disaster' – you need five deaths for that – but that is an insult to the miners and their families. Disaster it was.

This book is dedicated to miners and their families, with the hope that pit safety will become a top priority in future.

Jen Llywelyn
Ceredigion, 2013

Some of the Senghenydd colliers in 1913

List of pit disasters up to 1913

The greatest colliery disaster in the history of coal mining in Great Britain occurred at the Oaks Colliery, Stairfoot, near Barnsley, in 1866, when 360 men lost their lives and left over 1,000 dependents.

In 56 explosions in South Wales the estimated loss considerably exceeds 5,000.

1845	2 August	Cwmbach	26
1846	14 Jan.	Risca	35
1848	21 June	Victoria (Mon)	11
1849	11 August	Lletty Shenkin	52
1852	10 May	Dyffryn	64
1853	12 March	Risca Vale	10
1856	13 July	Cymmer	114
1858	13 October	Dyffryn	20
1859	5 April	Neath Chain	26
1860	1 Dec.	Risca	145
1862	19 Feb.	Gethin (Merthyr)	47
1863	17 Oct.	Margam	39
1863	24 Dec.	Maesteg	14
1865	16 June	New Bedwellty Pit (Tredegar)	36
1865	8 Dec.	Gethin	36
1865	20 Dec.	Upper Gethin	30
1866	16 June	New Bedwellty	25
1866	December	Oaks Colliery, Barnsley	360
1867	8 Nov.	Ferndale	178
1869	23 May	Llanerch	7
1869	10 June	Ferndale	60
1870	23 June	Llansamlet	19
1871	24 Feb.	Pentre	38
1871	4 October	Gelli, Aberdare	4
1872	10 January	Oakwood (Llynfi)	11
1872	2 March	Victoria	19
1872	8 March	Wernfach	18
1874	5 April	Abertillery	6
1874	24 July	Chas. Pit, Llansamlet	19
1875	4 Dec.	Powel Duffryn (New Tredegar)	22
1875	5 Dec.	Llan Pit, Pentyrch	12
1876	18 Dec.	Abertillery	20
1877	8 March	Worcester New Pit, Swansea	18

1878	11 Sept.	Abercarn	268
1879	13 January	Dinas	63
1880	15 July	Risca	120
1880	10 Dec.	Naval Colliery	101
1882	15 January	Risca	4
1882	11 Feb.	Coedcae	6
1883	1 Feb.	Coedcae	5
1883	21 August	Gelli	5
1884	16 January	Cwmavon	10
1884	28 January	Penygraig	11
1884	8 Nov.	Pochin, Tredegar	14
1885	24 Dec.	Mardy	81
1887	18 Feb.	Wattstown	37
1888	14 May	Aber (Tynewydd)	5
1890	20 January	Glyn Pit, Pontypool	5
1890	8 March	Morfa	67
1890	30 April	Llanerch Colliery	176
1892	11 March	Anderines Colliery, Mons, Belgium	153
1892	12 August	Gt. Western Coll.	61
1892	16 August	Park Slip, Tondu	116
1895	14 January	Audley, N. Staffs	77
1896	28 January	Tylorstown	57
1899	18 August	Llest (Garw)	16
1901	24 May	Universal Colliery, Senghenydd	81
1901	3 June	Fochriw	8
1901	10 Sept.	Llanbradach	8
1902	5 Sept.	Abertysswg	16
1902	23 May	Crow's Nest Pass, Fernie, B. Columbia	150
1903	30 June	Hanna, Wyoming (explosion and fire)	175
1905	21 January	Gowerto	10
1905	10 March	Clydach Vale	33
1905	11 July	Wattstown	119
1906	10 March	Courrieres, Pas de Calais	1,230
1908	4 March	Hamstead, Warwick	25
1908	17 August	West Stanley	168
1909	Deri	Bargoed	23
1910	11 May	Wellington	136
1910	21 Dec.	Pretoria, Bolton	344
1912	9 July	Cadeby, Yorks.	88
1913	Cadder	Lanarks.	22

[NOTE: this report, from Llais Llafur–Labour Voice *(18 October 1913) omits the disaster at Albion Colliery, Cilfynydd, on 23 June 1894, when 260 men died.]*

The first Senghenydd disaster
24 May 1901

William Thomas Lewis (later Lord Merthyr of Senghenydd) was born in Merthyr Tydfil on 5 August 1837, the son of Thomas William Lewis, the engineer of the Plymouth Ironworks in the town. He started school at the age of seven and finished when only twelve and a half, becoming an apprentice to his father. His determination to succeed in life was apparent even at that age, for after working a twelve-hour shift he would walk two miles to further his education, particularly in mathematics.

This determination started to pay off when he started his career in the employ of Lord Bute in 1855 as an assistant to the chief engineer of the Bute estate. His diligence in this job brought him to the attention of Lord Bute, and by the age of thirty he was appointed chief mineral agent to Lord Bute and controlled the mineral interests of over 128,500 acres. Part of his remit was to manage the Bute pits, and this must have spurred his desire to get into the thriving mining industry. He then continued to build up his assets until in the 1870s he grabbed the opportunity to branch out on his own. The Coedcae and Hafod pits at Trehafod were nothing exceptional, until Lewis took them over and used them as his base to build on of the most influential and profitable coal mining concerns in the world.

On the Hafod site he sank No. 1 and No. 2 Pits to the steam coal seams. He also sank the Bertie Pit and the Trevor Pit, and called the whole concern, modestly, Lewis Merthyr Collieries. The Lady Lewis pit was sunk in 1904, a mile up the valley from the main sinkings, and this completed his colliery. The total capacity for coal winding for these pits in 1901 was around 4,000 tons per nine-hour day.

In 1881 the Lewis Merthyr Navigation Collieries Limited was formed. By 1900 the title changed to Lewis Merthyr Consolidated Collieries Limited. The Universal Colliery at Senghenydd was acquired in 1905.

Lewis' exceptional energy and business acumen was seen both inside and outside of the mining arena. In 1873 Lewis controlled the Forest Iron and Steel Company, and later the International Coal Company and the Melingriffith Tin Plate Company. He became the Managing Director of the Cardiff Railway Company, and a director of the Rhymney Railway Company and the Newport Tin Plate Company. He became a Trustee for the Bute Estate in 1880 and was mainly responsible for Bute's development of Cardiff Docks and Railway.

His involvement on the industrial/political scene in south Wales was widespread. He was the main driving force behind the formation of the Coal-owners' Association in 1871, and the Sliding Scale Agreement in 1875; he also served on the Royal Commissions on Accidents in Mines and Coal Dust in Mines (1878), Mining Royalties and the Labour Commission (1889), Royal Commissions on Trades Disputes and Shipping Rings, and the Board of Trade Railways Inquiry. He was also President of the Mining Association of Great Britain, President of the Iron and Steel Institute, Chairman of the South Wales Board of Examinations for Mining Certificates, and a fellow of the Royal Geological Society.

In 1875 the South Wales Coalfield was in chaos. There was no organised structure between the individually egotistical and antagonistic coal-owners, and little cohesion within the workforce, particularly following the bankruptcy of the Amalgamated Association of Miners after the disastrous strike of 1875. Lewis coerced, persuaded and banged heads together on the owners' side and brought about what must be his finest achievement: unity under the banner of the Monmouthshire and South Wales Coal Owners' Association. Along with this he brought peace to the coalfield, for a while anyhow, by bringing in the Sliding Scale Agreement, whereby wages were controlled by the varying price of coal. This system showed the more ruthless side of Lewis' character, in that it was heavily biased against the workmen: any decrease in the price of coal and wages were dropped almost immediately, but when the price of coal increased it could take months before a pay rise was given. This system became so hated by the men that it was thrown out in 1905, and the South Wales Miners Federation was formed to negotiate on wages and other matters.

Lewis stood for Parliament for the Merthyr seat in 1880 but failed to get elected. He was knighted in 1885, made a baronet in 1896, made a freeman of Cardiff in 1905, and of Merthyr in 1908. He became Lord Merthyr of Senghenydd in 1911.

His wife died in 1902 and Lord Merthyr died on 27 August 1914. Their son, the Hon. Herbert Clark Lewis, succeeded to his title.

Syr William Thomas Lewis,
Lord Merthyr of Senghenydd,
the owner of the Universal Colliery

Only a few years after the first shafts were sunk at Senghenydd there were three explosions at the end of the night shift, around 5 a.m. on Friday 24 May 1901. The men in the last cage coming to the surface after the night shift were blown out of it. Those walking through the village first sent word to tell their families they were safe, then hurried back to the pit to see if they could help. Eighty-three men had been down the pit – a between-shifts group working overtime.

Edward Shaw, the pit manager, went immediately to see what the situation was. The Lancaster shaft's cages and lifting gear had been damaged in the explosion, but volunteers shifted the obstructions at the bottom of the shaft. By 11.30 a.m. rescue parties were in the pit. Despite a huge roof fall, they quite quickly found a man alive – William Harris, an ostler, lying alongside his dead horse. He was lifted to the surface, swathed with bandages, and taken to his home.

It was not thought that he would live.

The rescuers were elated by finding a man alive. But Harris was the only survivor, apart from two horses found further along. The explosion had been violent.

The train from Cardiff that evening brought forty coffins. Not nearly enough, as it turned out.

Thousands of people converged on the village, having walked from nearby mining communities – to help, and to support.

Sir William Thomas Lewis, the pit owner, was on holiday on the Côte d'Azur. He requested a progress report every four hours.

Over the next few days it became clear that there were no survivors – except for William Harris, who was still dangerously ill.

The bodies being recovered were all sickeningly mutilated, disfigured and burned. The ambulancemen, mortuary attendants and doctors did yeoman work to ensure their cleanliness and presentability for identification before they were placed in their coffins and carried home on the shoulders of their workmates and neighbours. In very many cases identification depended entirely on personal trivia like belt buckles, metal buttons, pocket watches, tins for 'twists' of tobacco, and such like.

Out of respect for the feelings for the bereaved families and for the stricken community as a whole, the dead were borne to their homes after dark; carried shoulder high by friends in a quiet lamplit procession through the hushed streets of the two villages.

At those homes the lasses of the Salvation Army, with their apposite motto of 'Blood and Fire', provided a woman's care and comfort for the sorrowing womenfolk, children and relations. They took charge of running homes, cooking meals, acting as foster mothers in caring for children, and provided solace for women broken under the weight of their grief.

The Valley of the Shadow (John H. Brown)

On Tuesday 28 May the funerals began. Five miners were carried on biers to Senghenydd station, where their coffins were put onto the 8.30 a.m. train: George Griffith was going home to Llanelli; John Harvey to Newport, Monmouthshire; John Davies to Newcastle Emlyn, and James James to Newport, Pembrokeshire. On the 9.30 a.m. train George Filer's body left for Treorchy. Then twelve funerals were held in the parish church of Eglwysilian, three miles out of Senghenydd. Unusually for Welsh funerals, there was no singing.

Over the next six weeks the rescue attempts continued. In the end eighty-one bodies (or what was left of them) were found. After this first Senghenydd explosion, fifty-seven women were widows, and 230 children fatherless.

William Harris lived, but was scarred for life, physically and mentally, and was convinced that he alone had been involved in the Senghenydd pit disaster of 1901.

Professor W. Galloway, a former Inspector of Mines, was asked by the Home Secretary to report on the Senghenydd explosion. He reported on 15 July 1901, saying that the Senghenydd pit was a hot and dusty pit, the dust being increased by the method used for loading the drams (trucks). Galloway strongly advised that roadways should be sprinkled with water to keep the dust down and reduce the danger of explosion. Fine coal dust piled in the roadways, and floating in the air, is an explosive mixture.

The inquest was held in October 1901. Various miners gave evidence, but it was clear that not all safety routines had been carried out, particularly with regard to the handing out of explosives. The jury concluded that the colliery had not been watered sufficiently, and called for parliament to make this compulsory. Another report considered that the pit management had not considered adequately the need to remove dust from the roadways.

As nobody had broken any existing laws, there was no leeway for a prosecution of the mine management or owners.

One of the main problems had involved the ventilation in the pits. Fans inside the pits drew out the stale and toxic air, sending it via the ventilation shafts placed at intervals along the coal workings. But in the event of a roof collapse, caused, for example, by an explosion, any trapped miners would need clean air to stay alive. In the event of a fire, the fire would consume all the oxygen, leaving any trapped men to die of asphyxiation. Therefore, if fans were reversed so as to send in new air, lives would be saved.

In 1911 the Coal Mines Act demanded that fans in all pits should be reversible, so that clean air could be provided in the case of emergency. This was required to be implemented by 1 January 1913.

The Universal Colliery owners requested an extension, and were given up to 30 September 1913 – a further nine months – to make their fans reversible.

But they did not make even that deadline ...

The second Senghenydd disaster
14 October 1913

'Aye, I was here in August 1895, when we struck the Six-Feet seam, down at 520 yards it was, beautiful seam it was. Senghenydd wasn't so big then, mind you, about 200 cottages and, believe it or not, three large hotels. I liked a pint in them days, see, we all did, until the revival of 1905 swept through the village. Couldn't move for chapels then – there were at least eight, of all sorts, Methodists, Baptists, Welsh Independents, United Reformed, Wesleyans, two Church of England places. Big solid buildings vying with each other for the glory of God, and for the most ornate insides, of course.

'We even had our own rugby team. Aye, Senghenydd RFC was formed in 1898, but rugby was seen as an evil sport that leads to drinking and fighting, so after the big revival in 1904 they couldn't get enough players, see. Until 1907, that is, when it started up again, and by 1911 we were winning things – Cardiff and District Champions, we were ... well, champions of the second division, anyway. We won the Lord Ninian Stuart Cup as well.

'Ah, those were the days, butty bach. I remember William Brace, the old union leader and MP, negotiating the price list for the Four-Feet seam. Little did we know the heartbreak that seam would bring to the village, and due to the cosmopolitan – that's a big word, bach! – make-up of the village, that heartbreak would echo through all of Wales, and England and Ireland as well. But at that time it was a good deal: we got one shilling and tuppence for a ton of clean large coal, plus the sliding scale percentage on top of that. The working places for a man and boy were to be 12 yards wide, with the coal 6 feet high. Could make a couple of bob out of that, except when you hit a patch of soft coal. Only paid you for large lumps, see. Boy, you ought to have seen the journeys of trams trundling out to the pit bottom, piled high to nearly twice their height with big lumps of coal, they was. Little did we know then that the lumps that fell off and were trampled by the horses and our boots into dust would help the killer flames to wipe out all life in the west side of the pit. Strange thing, life, ennit. They were good times, though, boy ... aye, they were. The pit hadn't been open long, like, about sixteen years, and the village was pretty new. Pretty wasn't exactly the word to describe it, though, but it was a good little place, stuck up the backside of a blind valley, like. Plenty of work in them days, mind you, plenty of work and a bit of money. People coming in from all ends to work here, from the west and mid Wales, aye, and even from England, like. Jobs for 'em all.

'Then it happened, didn't it, and it all went wrong ... Yes, it was only twelve years ago that eighty-two died at this pit in an awful explosion that left just one man alive underground. But you couldn't worry about that, could you. We had little choice really, you had to get stuck in and earn a living to support your family. There was no welfare state in those days – you couldn't worry about every little thing in life. You just got on with it. Unless there was a matter of principle at hand, and then you stood shoulder to shoulder with your butties to fight for a better life.'

The old man was right, those were relatively good times for the south Wales coalfield. The place was booming. In that year a staggering record 56,113,000 tons of coal had been dug out of the coal measures of south Wales, by a huge manpower of 225,213 miners. And that wasn't the peak year for manpower – that came in 1923, when 252,617 miners hacked away under the hills and valleys of southern Wales.

Suddenly it seemed everyone wanted to live and work at Senghenydd and its like. A population of a few hundred became many, many thousands. From being a Welsh-speaking area it gradually became an English-speaking one. The average wage in the south Wales coalfield for a miner was 6s 9d a shift (around 34p), compared with the English average of 6s 6d (32p). And thre'pence was a lot in those good old days. On top of this, the Minimum Wage Act for miners guaranteed them between 3s and 4s 7d in bad work places. Much, much better than working on a farm in, say, Wiltshire or Merioneth, and much better wages than could be offered in the geologically difficult Bristol and Somerset coalfields.

It wasn't all roses, though. The Senghenydd collier had to work an average of fifty-five hours per week, over six days, and the death rate was 3.71 to every 1,000 miners. For six days a week he descended into one of two dirty great big holes that used to swallow over 2,000 men every day, subject them to some of the toughest conditions a working man can endure, and then spit them back out, dirty and tired. Those holes were cruel masters, and the penalty for disobedience was often death or injury. They showed no compassion or favour to any man. They devoured without discrimination.

During May 1913 the 2,000 men in the Universal Colliery came out on strike over non-unionists working in the pits of south Wales. Along with 40,000 others, they struck for a few days until management agreed that only members of the South Wales Miners' Federation be employed in the pits of south Wales.

In the wider world, the Romanoffs celebrated 300 years on the Russian throne, little knowing what their fate would be a few years later. Australia was building its new capital, Canberra. The zipper was invented by a Swedish American. Pancho Villa's Mexican revolutionary troops took the town of Torreon; the construction of the Panama Canal was completed.

At home, on 4 June Emily Davison, a suffragette, ran out in front of the King's horse at the Epsom Derby and was killed (not until 1928 did all women get the vote).

And on 9 October, out in the cold, deep Atlantic, the *SS Volturno* caught fire and sank, with the loss of 130 people, mainly women and children.

'*Dere 'mlan, achan, coda*', shouts the Dad to his son. It was quarter to five in the morning, and they had to be down the pit by between 5.10 a.m. and 6 a.m. '*Paid ag anghofio dy frechdannau*'. The boy scrambled out of bed, dressed quickly and grabbed his sandwiches, before following his Dad out through the front door and into the crowd in the street, all heading in the same direction – to the

Universal Colliery. All sorts were there: the conscientious ones, who had been awake at 4 a.m. preparing for work, the scrabblers who didn't get up until 5 a.m, the reluctant ones pushed out of the door by wives or mothers, the good guys, some bad guys, but mostly in-the-middle guys. Colliers, boys, officials, hauliers, labourers, surface workers, timber men, all stumbled bleary-eyed from their beds, dressed, perhaps grabbed a cup of tea and gathered their bread, cheese and water, as they headed for the colliery. Their minds were preoccupied with the job in hand and the mundane routines of daily life.

Pit hooters wailed to get them out of bed. Boots clattered on the road. Some were talking low, some whistling. Most moved silently. There was no singing (that was for the movies).

At the top of the pit the miners' lamps, of the Cambrian type, were lit, then locked and given to the workmen. Down the pit they went then, all 950 of them. At the pit bottom they parted, some going back underneath their homes to work on the east side of the pit, the others to the west side. Again, on the way in, at the lamp-locking station, they had their lamps checked for safety. On the west side this was 440 yards in from the pit bottom. It was at this place that they met the firemen: Edward Jones, for the seventy-nine men going to the Pretoria District, D. Richards, for the twenty-three men in the East Ladysmith District, and Rees Thomas for the eighty-nine men in the West Ladysmith District. Evan Jones was in charge of the fifty men in the Kimberley District, while both W. Chidsey and Fred Williams managed the Bottanic District.

The firemen had been down the pit since 3.30 a.m. and had done their rounds to make sure that the workplaces were free of gas and safe to go to. Given the all-clear, the miners went off again, travelling well over 1,000 yards to their workplaces, in the dim pools of light given off their lamps – not so bad if you were in the front, but further back you were surrounded by dust clouds that made it very difficult to see. You depended on the men in front to warn you: 'Hole up!' for dangers on the floor, and 'Watch your head!' for sagging timbers.

On they went, into the dark depths of the mine, and disappeared as living beings ...

The steam hissed from the boilers, and chugged from the winding engine's cylinders, 6 feet long and 42 inches wide, that turned the pithead wheels and lifted two fully-laden trams of 2.5 tons of coal 1,849 feet every 38 seconds. The coal was tipped onto the screening plant, with big billows of coal dust covering everyone and everything, and then the empty trams were returned back down the shaft, to be filled again and again. The colliers loaded the coal into the trams, and then the haulier hitched his horse to them and brought them out to the point where twenty-four were made into a journey. Then, at the magnificent speed of 4 to 8 mph, compressed-air haulage engines brought the journey to the pit bottom ready for winding.

Everything worked as normal – that is, until 8.10 a.m., when those on the surface of the mine heard a bang. The manager, Edward Shaw, was in the lamp-room and immediately rushed over to the Lancaster Pit top. He found the banksman dead and the assistant banksman injured. The whole of the surface in the immediate vicinity of the pit top was wrecked.

Shaw rushed over to the York Pit and found that it was in order. Along with D. R. Thomas, an overman, he went down the pit – but after 50 yards they found the air foul with smoke and fumes. They returned to the top and found out that there was frantic signalling coming up from the pit bottom. They gathered others and went down again. When they were halfway down, the other cage was coming up, and there was the body of a man in it. He had been blown into the cage by the force of the explosion.

They got as far as the Six-Feet seam landing, and the cage became jammed by girders dislodged by the force of the explosion. They managed to free it, and reached the pit bottom. They found that the men from the east side were unharmed. They first tried to go into the east side, but the raging fires forced them back. The same thing happened on the west side, where the ventilation doors had been blown off and the timbers were on fire. They put out the fire and managed to reach the bottom of the Lancaster Pit, where they found Ernest Moses alive.

On the other side of the pit they found another five or six

hitchers, who were still alive, but they all died later.

Shaw and another man worked their way along the Main East Level. Shaw stated, 'It was exactly like looking into a furnace ... and all the timber, so far as I could see from there on, was all ablaze ... every collar [wooden roof support] blazing in front of me for 20 or 30 yards'. The roof of the roadway was still intact, but Shaw saw 'that the laggings were just beginning to break down'.

By that time the pits had been cleared and the men from the east side workings were brought to the surface.

W. H. Lansbury was one of the fortunate ones. Having gone down the pit at 7.50 a.m. he was making his way into the workings when he heard a dull thud from behind him, and was covered in dust. He lost his light, and fell to the ground. He called to the engineman, who said, from nearby, that he was all right. He then turned back towards the pit and began to feel his way out, in total darkness. As he neared some closed ventilation doors they crashed open, and there was a great rush of air. He managed to get to the pit bottom and collapsed.

Thomas Jones was another lucky man. He was working in another coal seam 27 yards below the disaster seam, but even he 'heard a roar or rumble ... coming from some distance, and then a terrific and distinct bang'. Sydney Gregory heard two heavy thuds, and the air became still, followed by a cloud of coal dust 'as thick as a fog'. Later on, the fireman came and told them to get out. 'It was awful. Timber was crackling and falling, and we could hardly bear the heat and the foul air.'

At the village people began to realise that something terrible had happened, and women started to rush towards the pillars of smoke above the pits. The relatives and friends of those underground packed into the pit top. Soon others, from outside the village, started to arrive, some concerned about their friends and loved ones, some to watch, and many men from other mines to offer their services as rescuers. The crowd became so large that it spread from the pit top to the surrounding hillsides and even the onset of nightfall failed to budge it. A newspaper reporter commented:

I have never seen so silent a throng. The absence of noise was extraordinarily impressive. Few words were spoken by that vast crowd as the hours toiled slowly on ... the women particularly seemed to be steeling themselves against the knock-down blows which are the lot of miners' wives ...'

Group of anxious women and children

Poem of the survivor

*This is not by any reckoning great poetry. It is included
because it so effectively recreates the terror and horror of
Archie Dean, stuck deep underground, trying desperately to get
out, and to help his 'butties', and then the relief of rescue.*

1.   It was a little after eight on Tuesday morning
     When a dreadful sound was heard,
     The sound, came from a pit head,
     People; wondered what had occurred,
     Then, soon; the news began to spread
     Through the small village of Senghenydd;
     People rush from all direction,
     Over hill and valley low,
     To the sad pit that in destruction;
     And their dear ones down below.

2.   Then there was no time to lose; not a moment
     To rescue those who was alive,
     And; to bring to the surface
     From the dreadful burning mine,
     Husband son and brothers
     Who; were down there
     What a sad story to tell,
     They were down in the bowel of the earth,
     Which was like a burning hell.

3.   Then the manager with others;
     Who descended the shaft
     At that fateful hour,
     Not knowing the lives, that were ending
     But doing the best in their power.
     Anxious hearts eager eyes; were waiting
     Waiting, for the report;

At last the sad answer came
East side safe, the west side no hope.

4.   The battle began to fight the fire
And to rescue those who were alive
And bring them to the surface
From the dreadful burning mine
Doctor and Nurses were ready
Ready to their task
To ease the pain of the injured
Who had met that terrible blast
The sight it was heart rending
As they were brought from the mine
Prayers to God from every heart
To those who were brought up alive.

5.   I was working that day
When this happened in the mine
Doing my job as a miner
I was working at the coal fact that time
The shock I had that morning
Was a whirlwind of dust through the coalface
Which I never experienced before boys
It was like on a death race
Others they had felt it
And to you I will explain
They ask me what has happened
I said it may be a fall on the main

6.   We, all, then, made for the intext ('intext' means an airway)
The nearest way to the pit shaft
Not knowing what had really happened
Until we smelt the smoke
Then we knew something serious had happened
And wondering the best thing to do
So we, tried the main way

But could not get through
We wandered back and forward
With scarves to our mouths

7. To keep out the deadly after damp
And praying to find a way out
My little helper was in front of me
I was close behind
Such a shock I never experienced
As a miner of years in the mine

8. Backward and forward we faced it
Although we were all in despair
Longing to see daylight again
And breathe the pure air
My legs were getting weak
For there I must have fell
Not knowing; what was passing
Down; in this terrible burning hell.

9. When I came to myself,
Hours there I must have laid
My thoughts went to my homestead
To my wife and children dear
Praying to God to help me
And guide me and preserve

10. A lamp was still alight
It was like diamonds to my eyes
It was put down by a comrade
Overcome by after damp had died
He was grasping a jack of tea
I took it from his arms which I sipped
Which was a godsend to me

11. With this precious tea jack
    I on my hands and knees did crawl
    Passing some dear comrades
    Who were gone beyond recall
    I came across two lads
    Who were still alive
    I gave them a drink
    From the precious tea jack
    Which helped them to revive

12. Leaving those two comrades
    I on my hands and knees did crawl
    Passing on my way dead horses
    And men beyond recall
    I then stopped and sat down
    It was on the main parting
    My back ached frightfully
    For the horrors of the scene
    Are stamped on my memory
    Giving up all hope ever to see
    My wife and children three
    Then the lamp went out
    That made it worse for me

13. How long I sat there
    I really, do not know
    Later I saw light coming
    It was the rescue party
    Who had risked their lives
    To save their comrades
    Who had been
    Twenty two hours
    Down the dreadful burning mine

I am only a Senghenydd Survivor
The sad story here I have told
It was the sad day of the 13th of October
When the small village of Sengenydd was mourning
It's many years past since it happened
And the dear ones are laid in the graves
So that concludes my sad story
One of the eighteen men saved

We raise our hats and many mourn
To the men who volunteer and risk their lives
To save their fellow workmen
God bless them everyone
Also the Barggo first aid Ambulance men
Also Doctor Thomas of Barggo
With the Agent of the Aber Collieries
Who work their way over falls
Through pot hole of gases
To get into the Bertanic District
Which was down the one North
To get to the intext from that end
Which was the only way to get there
The intext was only 11 yards long
Long as my heading was opening out to the one north
While Ben Hill was opening out to the one north to Bertanic
As I think it was owing through the intext
Being only 3 feet wide 3 feet high saved us from having the full
Blast so I give my thanks to the Collier agent who planned and
Said we will make all effort from that end to get there
And they saved the eighteen that was alive there
But only Pot Luck and just in time.

A typescript narrative, in verse form, concerning the Senghenydd mining disaster, 14 October 1913, written by the donor's late father Archibald Dean, one of only eighteen survivors found in the Bottanic district after the explosion.

National Library of Wales, ex1671
Donation June 1995 (Mrs V. P. Hames, Strood, Kent)

Carrying some of the miners' bodies out of the cage

'Raging Sepulchure of Senghenydd'

by a Special Correspondent

Western Mail, Tuesday 15 October 1913

Between Cardiff and Senghenydd there are four stations, and between them slow trains have been dragging all day. Since the first news of the disaster was sent over the wire early this morning the trains have been full, crammed full, with silent men and pale women with swimming eyes.

Drawn up at a platform they have seen an engine and a single carriage rattle past at intervals, bearing to the hospital at Cardiff men who may yet die before they enter its doors. Finally, after what seems an interminable journey, the train clanks into Senghenydd and stops, and they plod patiently along the black, unlevel road up to where, in the fork of the valley, the stacks and sheds of the great colliery stand out grimly.

The uneven roads are full of people – more silent men, more women with drawn faces and moist eyes. The slopes of the mountains – either side green enough, despite the blackness of the village – are spotted with groups. Police begin to be in evidence, good-naturedly keeping the road clear to the great tragedy.

Then the gaunt, straddling mechanism of the huge winding wheels, a general ugly confusion of wire and wood and brickwork, feathery tufts of steam sizzling here and there; continually, black greasy mud underfoot, a silent crowd, with constant movement in the middle of it, nurses with the Red Cross on their breasts, ambulance men, motor cars, more police, cinematograph operators ... over all a grey sky and a faintly acrid reek in the air, like rotting wood. That is the taste of the fires below.

It is terrible to think that underneath us as we stand, even though the scene be hideous, 400 men are lying twisted in a hell of smoke and fume and poisonous gases. There is nothing to see yet, save a monotonous procession of men with the red grenades which are to fight the raging devils below with chemicals. They brought up eleven corpses this morning – you can see them in that shed at the furthest end of the row, poor cold, mangled fragments of flesh which make you physically sick to see, so shattered and torn are they.

No more rescue work can be done till the brave, blackened fire-fighters have conquered in the struggle below our feet ... One of them, perspiring, coal-black, pushes into the shed, where there is a fire burning brightly and where food and drink may be hastily despatched.

'Well?' says a grey bearded man to him.

'No more, doctor,' he says, wiping his face. 'Fire and smoke worse than this morning. But I think we're getting at them in the west – don't know if they're alive or dead,' and he pushes out again.

In this way the grey autumn afternoon passes. The crowd thickens, the workers come and go, until by five o'clock (God be praised!) there is news that the fire is under control at last and the rescue work may begin.

Waiting for news – one of W. Benton's iconic photographs

The crowd is very quiet. The men, apathetic and stolid in the face of Death, a frightful death which may come to each of them in his turn and sweep them to destruction, converse hardly at all, and then in low voices.

It is the women who talk, not violently or idly, but with a sense, perhaps, that talk will save them from going mad. They tell how in one house a father has been swept away, in another a son, in another two sons and two brothers, in yet another a husband, two sons, and two brothers. They talk also of women who have fainted before the feared news was told to them, seeing death in the informant's eyes. They tell of young lads, pallid with fright under their outer skin of coal grime, collapsing in the rescuers' arms. They tell of a woman who has drowned the memory of a dead husband in drink, and who raved and shouted and cursed at all things in heaven and earth in her madness ... But for the most part they are stonily quiet, showing only the torture they are enduring by the lines under the eyes and the strained look of despair.

The Huts, Senghenydd – the houses closest to the pit

So the day wears wearily away in bleak Senghenydd, and still there are 400 men, by this time beyond all hope, dead in the raging sepulchure of flames and smoke underground. And of all this, there is only the faint acrid smell of the air to paint the whole horror on the imagination.

'An Unforgettable Experience'

from Ups and Downs,
recollections of Walter Haydn Davies,
who as a boy of thirteen went to work in a pit,
and later became Headmaster of Bargoed Grammar School

The Aber Valley was really an offshoot of the main Rhymney valley about five miles north-west of Caerphilly. At the head of this valley stood Senghenydd, with Abertridwr a little lower. Senghenydd was like most other mining villages, many of its houses clinging limpet-like to the mountain side, having shot off at right-angles from the main road running down the valley parallel to both railway and river. Nestling in a hollow slightly above the village of Senghenydd was the Universal Colliery, surrounded on three sides by high bleak hills which seemed to frown upon the havoc industry had wrought on their valley below. Before the sinking of the colliery and the urban development that followed, this valley must surely have been as unspoilt as any to be found in rural Wales, and when the explosion occurred here it was as if nature had decided on its revenge against man's handiwork, which had raped and despoiled this ancient untarnished landscape.

On this beautiful October day, this industrial valley, basking in the sunshine, still managed to look strikingly attractive, its fields and hillside glistening with a rich, brilliant, verdant green, the slated roofs of the houses below too reflecting the brilliancy of the blue sky above, the total effect heightened by the fact that the trees had not yet lost their foliage, so that it seemed as if the valley had still retained much of its rural splendour.

But this tranquility of the telescopic view was in vivid contrast to what was to be disclosed near to hand, for as we got nearer we saw suddenly the ill-fated colliery with its mangled pit gear. The tragedy was obvious, for the pithead and surface works were crowded with men, women and children standing motionless, with groups scattered about the hillsides, watching and praying. There was little display of emotion – no hysterical weeping – but the very grimness in the demeanour of the people added poignancy to the spectacle.

The scene at the top of the pit

I saw no flames shooting up to the sky from the pit shaft, none of the fireworks display I had imagined – only a sunlit scene.

This contrast of beauty and tragedy brought home to me that a colliery disaster, unlike a summit place on fire or the results of a tornado, reveals little of its damage on the surface, for its inferno rages in the depths below the earth.

Still, what an unforgettable imprint on my mind came when we joined the crowd of onlookers. Amongst them was a young woman with a shawl over her shoulders, sobbing bitterly and crying out softly, 'Mam! Mam! He will never come back no more'. The white-haired mother silently led her distraught daughter along the narrow pathway down the tip to her home. I watched them, stricken by the tragic picture they made.

There was an air of expectancy as the great wheels above the colliery shaft began to turn, taking the cages up and down the pit. When the wheels stopped turning there was an agony of waiting before the stretcher-men came along, carrying the dead bodies of those who had just been brought up the shaft. As they passed, one could hear the murmured laments of the onlookers. 'Poor dabs! They were only 30 yards from safety!' In fact, these casualties struggled through about 900 yards of a living inferno in an atmosphere of dense fumes and afterdamp, to reach the main return and safety, only to drop dead at the last moment.

We moved amongst the crowd, glancing at distraught faces, listening to voices thick with despair. A reference made here to the luck of an absentee miner, or there to the children of a missing one; a quick calculation to ease numbed brains.

Hopes of a miracle occurring at Senghenydd that day were soon dashed when news came that the rescue team had fought their way through to the Mafeking district, to find nothing but dead bodies about the place. Yet hope dies hard, and even after such despairing news a kind of false optimism spread that things might possibly get better, a feeling which led to many rumours throughout the day. It was said that the rescuers had heard knockings, but there was no

Some of the damage on the surface

40

truth in the report. In the tense atmosphere the Welshman's proclivity for the macabre and supernatural came into play. A fantastic story soon spread that a phantom luminous miner had been seen down the pit just ahead of one rescue party, beckoning them to follow him, and then had pointed to the dead bodies. Boyish curiosity made us edge nearer and nearer to the colliery shaft in order to see the cages go up and down. We saw the rescue teams from other areas entering the cages carrying with them the safety lamps, a lifeline, a stretcher, and a canary in a cage. Canaries react more quickly to the presence of gas than men.

Towards evening clouds began to gather and we had to begin our long trek homewards. As we climbed the hillside we stopped occasionally to mingle with the various scattered groups of people who had remained at certain vantage points throughout the day, listening to their comments and observations about the grim tragedy below.

As we climbed the mountain it began to drizzle and darkness came softly and we were anxious to get home. For the first time we thought of our parents and their anxiety about us. 'It's as well,' I reflected, 'that when Twm called for me this morning to go to school he mentioned that immediately after school we might go up to his uncle's farm. Mam will probably think I am at Twm's house.'

As we neared the mountain top we were joined by a middle-aged man, who, because he had those tell-tale blue marked scars on his hands and face usual to men of that occupation, was obviously a miner. The scars were igrained as if drawn with a blue indelible pencil – a reminder that the pit was no respecter of persons. Such marks were the result of flesh wounds sustained whilst working underground where minor cuts and bruises are so commonplace that the miner treats them lightly at the time they happen, and instead of leaving his place of work for treatment he carries on working, allowing the coal dust to form a kind of plaster over the scored skin.

This miner now walked along with us. He asked, 'Been to Senghenydd, have you, boys bach?'

41

'Yes!' we chorused.

'What a terrible disaster,' he said. 'Do you know the force of the explosion was so strong that the banksman working on the pithead had his head blown right off!'

'Good God!' exclaimed Ianto. 'What a dreadful thing to happen!'

'Yes,' the man assured us, 'one chap lucky enough to be brought up alive said the explosion was so loud that it was like the crack of doom'. He paused, then warned: 'You watch, the coal owners will soon be saying that the miners themselves were responsible for the disaster. They'll find some poor fellow with fags in his pocket and they'll say straight away, someone must have been smoking. Crawshay of Cyfarthfa started that lie', he added scathingly. 'He'd think the worst of them; for he treated miners like dogs, he did. We miners know damn well that by lighting a fag underground we are just committing suicide and murdering a fellow-worker in the process. So why should we do such a senseless thing?'

The Deep of the Earth

A novel by Luther Thomas,
published by Macmillan, 1956

['Maindy' is clearly a representation of Senghenydd]

It was just like any other working morning.

With the self-same howl, like some giant wolf, the pit hooter called forth another day almost before the last had ended. From the high terraces on the mountain sides to the floor of the valley, one after the other in crazy fashion the lights went on. And some beyond the valley, as there were men who came fair distances to work at the Maindy pits.

Doors slammed and hob-nailed boots beat out the familiar staccato along the roads to the pits.

Here a silent pair. There a laughing group of boys.

Was that a song so early?

Pale white faces in black surround.

Out of the darkness a train whistled.

Shoulder to shoulder now on the last rise to the main gates. Some silent men who would know a deeper silence. Some jesters who would never joke again. Boys who would never be men. Men who would never be old men. Old men who would not die peacefully.

The hiss of escaping steam to drown their voices as the wheels begin to turn. Down goes the first cage. That's the Number Two pit going now. Up and down, down and up. To the heights, and to the depths. Down to a lamp-invaded blackness – and what? Up to another dawn.

A watch that was taken from one of the bodies – the time of the explosion is frozen on its face

Just another day. To the great wide world beyond the valley, some tons of black shining rock, seeming inanimate. To the men of Maindy, life, aye, and death. But they did not measure it as such. Let no man say they did. Men have to die. They knew. But not like this.

William had been working on the night shift for some weeks. He would come up the pit round about five to five-thirty in the morning. He stayed longer than usual in the office this morning. He usually got home before Gwyneth and the children were up. He would light the fire and put the kettle on before going to call them. This morning they were already up when he walked in. Glyn and Ceridwen were out in the back washing under the tap. They joked about the cold water.

'Good for you,' William had said. 'Keep your skin clear.'

As Gwyneth got the breakfast ready, William filled the big bucket and the iron kettle with water and placed them one each side of the fire to heat up ready for his bath. He scrubbed his hands under the tap and took his stool into the kitchen to sit down to breakfast. He

43

A temporary mortuary following the disaster

Some of the 5,000 keeping vigil at the top of the pit

always gave the children the impression of a black man with a pair of white gloves, white with streaks of blue where the coal dust had permanently marked old cuts.

Gwyneth was seated in front of the fire toasting some bread when it happened. The very house rocked. Water slopped over from the bucket into the fire with an angry hiss, and white dust floated about the kitchen. Gwyneth's face went white and the children ran to her in fright.

William was shocked to a standstill. He hadn't been in Maindy when the last explosion happened, but he sensed that something awful had come.

'Oh, *Duw Mawr*, what is it, Will?' shouted Gwyneth.

But Gwyneth knew. She had been there twelve years before when the valley rocked like this.

'Oh, William, cariad, it's the pit, it's the pit!' cried Gwyneth, and she rushed to William's work-grimed arms.

William gently forced her to a chair and tore himself away in a rush to the front door. From where he stood on top of the steps he could see hundreds of people running from all directions up towards the pits. He almost jumped down the steps and took hold of one young woman who was running and shouting at the top of her voice.

'Steady on, my girl, tell me what has happened.'

She didn't want to stop. She dragged her arm from his grasp, but William caught her again, a little roughly this time.

'Hisht, girl, what is it?'

'Oh, Duw, listen to him,' she shouted. 'Don't you know, man? It's the pit. There's been an explosion.'

William ran back to the top of the steps to where Gwyneth and the children were standing and told them to stay in the house until he got back. And as he was he joined in that headlong rush to the pits. There were men like him, still in their pit clothes from the night shift, men who knew him as Will Evans the overman. He knew no more than they did. He passed women, some running as fast as the men, with shawls and aprons or a coat thrown hastily over the shoulders. There were older men and women, husbands and fathers, mothers and sisters, all joined up in that marathon of death.

Long before he got to the gates William could see the pithead sheaves all smashed up in a twisted mass of steelwork and corrugated sheets and tangled wire ropes.

They were carrying Evan Jones the banksman away as William got to the top of the Number One pit. He was dead, killed by the force of the explosion as it reached the top of the pit.

'*Nefoedd Mawr*, Will, it's happened again.'

'Hello, Ben, where is Mr Jervis?'

'I'm not sure, but I think he went down the pit with Nick Pugh and a few others. *Duw Mawr*, mun, I was by here when it happened.'

William ran to the Number Two pit. He got there as the cage broke the surface. Nick Pugh stepped out. Behind, William could see men, injured men. He could hear the groans above the medley of noises round him.

'Hello, Nick. What's the position?'

'Hello, Will,' said Nick, but William thought it didn't look like the Nick he knew.

Nick shook his head. '*Duw Mawr*, Will.'

'Where's Mr Jervis?'

'He's down there. He wants this cage down as fast as we can get these poor beggars out. There's more down there, Will. A lot more. Oh *Nefoedd*, come, Will. Come on, chaps, over by here.'

There were countless willing hands – willing indeed? Desperate, clamouring, beseeching hands – to drag those injured from that cage of hell. It was oly seconds before the men were laid on stretchers, mostly improvised out of nothing, it seemed. Nearly thirty there were in that first cage. Then down it went, sucked to the bloody depths.

'We were in the lamp-room, Will,' said old Nick. 'Talking about the antics of his oldest boy, he was. Aye, Mr Jervis. Then it happened. *Duw Mawr!* I shall never forget the look on his face as long as I live. I was froze, mun. He seemed to stare at me as if I knew something about it. The next second he was off, shouting like some madman at the top of his voice'.

Old Nick wasn't a talker. 'Never know what that bloody northman is thinking', was what most people said. Yes, a quiet chap was Nick the North. But now he was talking as if he could never stop.

'I've seen hell, Will, down there.'

The upcoming cage broke the surface as Nick talked. Again it was a matter of seconds, but it seemed longer. Men jumped to open the gates almost before it came to rest. There were some injured men who insisted on walking out unaided, pointing inarticulate messages to those behind.

'*Nefoedd Mawr*, Nick, there's fire down there. Look at them, Nick, look at them.'

'I said hell, Will. It's over on the West Side that the fires seem to be. They were getting over there when I came up.'

William put his hands under a man's arms to lift him. William's hands were scorched. His heart was scorched. The clothing fell away in dust. He was gripping flesh. Hot dry flesh. The man groaned pitifully. He died in William's arms.

Away sorrow; away tears and remorse. You can come later.

'Water.'

William turned to the man who cried for water. Those swollen lips. Those sightless eyes. That face. Face? Those beseeching hands. Hands? And yet he could lift the bottle to his mouth. Mouth?

Nefoedd Mawr, he's dead. He was saved.

On went the bottle. Water, water. The cry went up. Here to quench an aching thirst, below to quench the burning fire.

'I'm going down, Nick.'

William stayed down the pit for the whole of that first terrible day and all through the following night. Others too. Right up to the beginning of the afternoon of the second day. He was then ordered home, but to return that same evening.

As with the darkness underground, so with the daylight now. He lingered, looking down over the railings at the side of the pit, getting used to the daylight. He looked down on to the rows of full and empty coal wagons. The rock on which their lives had been built. Black, but clean. A power.

It was cold indeed after those hours of heat below ground. He shivered. He was without his jacket still.

He felt a heavy overcoat being placed over his shoulders. He turned to see a chap he hardly knew. 'No indeed, man, you need it as much as I do.'

'Bring it up when you come back.'

'No, no, I'll be home in a jiffy now.'

'Take it. I'm inside by there.' And he pointed to the carpenter's shop which had been quickly turned into a sort of mortuary.

'It's not cold in there, somehow,' he said. 'What about some hot tea, eh?'

'No, thank you, I'll get home now. Thank you for the coat. I'll bring it back this evening. So long now.'

William moved off to the gates and to the road outside. People rushed to him, as they did to all who passed out. They were mostly women there.

Where is this one? Where is that one? Have you seen so-and-so? Is my husband down there? Some plucked his sleeve as he made his way through. He answered he knew not what. He looked round him and saw the crowds stretching far and wide. He was lost in the crowd.

Dan Lloyd and the Senghenydd School Log

Dan Lloyd was appointed Headmaster of the Mixed School in 1898. When the boys' and girls' schools were built he took the headship of the Boys' School, which he held until 1925. His pupils reported that he was 'a man of outstanding ability and personality'; his Log entries are full of compassion for the home conditions of the pupils, and also with battling bad attendance and truancy, and attempting to maintain the grant for the school, which was based on average attendance. At one point Dan Lloyd was appointed one of the 'Overseers of the Poor' in Senghenydd.

Mrs Lloyd died in October 1909 (the school closed for her funeral), and his only son Reginald, who played rugby for

Senghenydd and Oxford University, was mentioned in despatches before dying of wounds in the First World War.

Dan Lloyd's successor in 1925 had grown up in Senghenydd, and later married Dan Lloyd's daughter Florrie.

After the 1901 explosion Dan Lloyd recorded in the Log:

4 June 1901
Among the victims of the holocaust were 10 fathers who among them had 12 boys in this Department.

7 June 1901
The gloom and awful results of the explosion accounts for the lowest attendance this year.

This is his log entry on the day of the second disaster:

14 October 1913
Appalling disaster at our local colliery. The town bereaved and frantic with grief. School closed.

Dan Lloyd's school, and the Infants' and Girls' Schools, remained closed until Monday 20 October. At the Infants' School about a third of the pupils turned up, and at the Girls' School 28 per cent. But the Boys' School had to close again. On Tuesday 21st the schools opened again; more infants and girls arrived, but there were still very few boys.

Due to the disaster 489 children were left fatherless (thirty-nine of whom were born after 14 October), and twenty orphans. It is hard to imagine the task of the school teachers working with the local children in the aftermath of the explosion. However, in the first half of 1914 Dan Lloyd recorded with pleasure that the school had beaten Caerphilly School in a baseball match; and reported that all the Irish pupils were absent on St Patrick's Day (17 March).

The post-war years of Dan Lloyd – without his wife or his son – are not recorded, but it seems Senghenydd was fortunate to have the services of this compassionate man to look after their boys in these difficult decades.

Rescuers

The first of the Mines Rescue teams arrived at 10 a.m. with much-needed breathing apparatus. Priority had been given to connecting up water pipes so that the fires could be put out. This was completed by 11 a.m. Still the fires raged on. It was agreed by all concerned to put up 'stoppings', that is, block off the fires and starve them of oxygen.

It was not until that night that all the confusion was sorted out. The rescue had been hampered by the lack of ventilation, lack of water, and lack of rescue equipment, and the explorers did not enter the Bottanic District until 10 p.m. They found the first man at 11.30 p.m., and brought out eighteen alive by the morning.

Watts Morgan was one of the rescue team. His story goes:

We were proceeding slowly, after the fire had abated somewhat, when we found a boy groaning. He was very weak and all but gone. We applied artificial respiration for two hours, and eventually brought him round. We were naturally delighted, and gave a sort of cheer when we came across them. We came across altogether eighteen men who were alive ... we went round a number of other districts but were finally driven back by the fumes. Most of the eighteen were in a bad plight when they were brought to the bank between 2 and 3 in the morning.

One of the rescued men, Ernest Jones, said:

We heard a loud report from the direction of the Lancaster Pit and realised that something serious had happened. I was working in the Bottanic district, and a number of us got together. We gradually moved forward, but with great difficulty. We got separated one by one until at last only I and another man, whom I did not know, were left. He made an attempt to get on, but after going a few yards he had to give up. The air was heavily laden with fumes from burning timber, and I could not realise what was the cause, though I was conscious that something serious beside the explosion had taken place. At midday I sat down on the side of the road and gave up all hope. I was unable to proceed any further. I must have lost consciousness, for I remember nothing more until I saw the rescue party.

Also saved were a father and his two sons. George Moore, the father, was a haulier, and was working near his sons when the explosion happened. He heard a loud report and was 'stifled' for a time, and his horse was killed. The three of them tried to get out of the district, but were forced back, and decided to wait. Each of them lost consciousness for periods of time.

A rider called Williams told the newspapers:

I was going down on a journey, riding on the rope, when the blast came and blew me off, knocking me onto my back. I knew it was an explosion, because the journey jumped the road and stopped. My lamp went out and I was in darkness ... I tried to make my way back to the pit but the afterdamp was too strong ... I was very giddy, and I suppose I must have lain down. I don't think I was conscious all the time, but I woke up and saw the rescue party and their lights.

The rescue party was a balance of all the parties involved in mining in those days. There were some from the owners of some of the mines, some from the South Wales Miners Federation, including Watts Morgan, then you had someone from government, the colliery officials, a doctor, and of course the Rhymney Valley Rescue Brigade. With the ventilation restored, they followed the fresh air route into the workings via the No. 1 North Road, passing four bodies who seemed to have died from carbon monoxide poisoning, plus one living horse. The Bottanic

District itself was reached and they found the body of a haulier who had been hurled over a tram by the force of the explosion. They then passed the body of a fireman as they reached the working face, where most of the survivors were found.

Members of the rescue teams coming up from the pit,
where the fires were still burning

Newspaper reports

Albert Victor Williams was on a rescue team. He was only eighteen, an apprentice carpenter at a pit in Pontypridd. He told a reporter:

I belonged to the pit Ambulance Brigade so it was only natural that I should volunteer to help. A group of us tramped five miles over the mountain to Senghenydd and there were thousands at the pit head when we assembled in the carpenter's shop waiting for instructions and watching loads of fire extinguishers being lowered into the pit.

I then joined a rescue party about to descend the pit, but first, like every other man, I made a will. Mine read, 'I bequeath my property and effects to my next of kin, my father, Thomas Benjamin Williams, 42 Pantygraigwen Road, Pontypridd'. I put it in a sealed envelope and dropped it into a box as I moved towards the cage.

Miners and the doctors
Llais Llafur/Labour Voice
Saturday 25 October 1913

There are heroes and unselfish characters in all ranks and professions, and the medical profession, says a correspondent, has its full share. In South Wales the medical men have rendered ungrudging and frequently heroic service at every colliery disaster, and these services have not been given exclusively by those practising within the colliery districts, but have been contributed by doctors from far and near, who have hastened to the scene to do what they could. No wonder that the doctors are beloved by the miners.

The County Echo [Pembrokeshire] was proud to report, on 6 November, that two Pembrokeshire mining engineers had figured prominently in the rescue work at Senghenydd: Mr John Rees from Alltypistyll, near Rhydwilym, General Manager of the Windsor Colliery, Abertridwr, and Cllr Harry Jenkins, Manager of the same colliery. They went down with the first rescue party on 14 October:

They were underground for several hours, and did deeds of heroism which deserve the highest praise. Neither of the two heroes left the colliery premises for about fifty hours, and at the end of which time they were compelled to go home and seek rest, as they were too exhausted to give an account of their daring and strenuous experiences to the Pressmen present. They have not only headed rescue parties, but have also laboured like Trojans at repairing work, and were always ready to do whatever they possibly could. Their names will always be honoured in connection with the tragic disaster as two of the bravest men that ever descended a coal mine. ... Mr Jenkins, on one occasion, was slightly overcome by gas, but on assistance being rendered, he soon recovered, and was able to continue the dangerous work in company with Mr Rees. Their experiences at the explosion would fill a column which would be treasured by everyone, as it would contain the deeds of two who have risked their lives times out of number without the slightest thought of praise or recompense.

Rescuing was dangerous. The shafts and tunnels had been damaged extensively by the explosion and the fire, and there were pockets of poisonous gas around every corner. One party ran into one of these clouds and struggled towards fresh air, but collapsed, and were found just in time by another party of rescuers.

Letter from Will Fisher to his cousin Charlie Mason

Twyn Cottages
Beddau
Caerphilly
Glam

Wednesday, November 11th 1913

Dear Charlie,
Your letter of the 8th to hand.

A month has gone since this terrible calamity occurred; we have recovered 165 bodies so far; and 280 still remain below in that deadly atmosphere. Every possible difficulty faces us; roads blocked here and there by falls of roof, ventilation doors blown down, thus disorganising ventilation altogether; consequently Mining Experts from all over the country are here devising ways and means of carrying ventilation in small sections by erecting brattice sheets here, and doors there, to enable us to penetrate the workings and snatch away the bodies.

Four shifts of six hours each continually keep the work going. We follow the air-current, level down falls, erect temporary timber making it safe to travel, then carry away the bodies. At times the gas, Carbon-Monoxide, beats us and we have to clear out for a shift or two; retiring towards pit bottom, repairing and opening out the mains till the ventilation is right again.

Three weeks ago we entered the Kimberley Dist., worked our way along a mile and half of main road, but failed to reach the 'Coal Faces' where most of the men are employed; - we passed numbers of bodies on the way (traffic men), lying all shapes; faces downwards on the road, or sitting on the roadside, a haulier blown under his tram, the horse lying across the tram, one man buried by a fall, his foot sticking out. Another caught by the full blast, dismembered, his head yards away. A Haulage Engineman sitting behind his brakes, huddled up, his head sunk on his breast. All killed instantly.

Some of us were levelling falls, just making a small passage for people to travel over. After some two hours my mate complained of feeling unwell and I felt a severe headache coming on, and a sensation akin to alcoholic intoxication creeping over me; the Afterdamp was on us. So we sat on the roadside; after a while the Advance Party came staggering back, 'Try and get out boys'. And what a job we had; struggling on a few yards, then resting; the stronger helping the weaker.

Were it not for the Rescue Brigade with their Oxygen Apparatus, who came in after us, we would never have got out alive; am enclosing a press cutting. I have always had a craze for new experiences; of late I've been busy with these. This is the third time I have faced Death; but this time there was no excitement; my brain was more or less active, and my interest in unusual phenomena was aroused; how would these men I knew so well, act under the circumstances. It was a verification of our Determinist position that man is good by nature. No-one failed in his Duty. I noticed no individual scramble for himself. All or none must be saved.

It was a week after this before we could enter this Dist. Again. We fetched the bodies off the Main Road, but failed to reach the 'Faces' and the colliers remain there yet.

Last week we managed to explore one of the four Districts, Ladysmith, on the new plan of ventilating a small section, exploring it, then letting it fill with gas again; shifting the air current on to another Section. We cleared the whole District of bodies, with the exception of five, who must be buried under the large falls, which will be cleared later. We locate the bodies under the smaller falls by the stench, digging them out (a horrible job), but the big falls bury them too deep – that is a titbit for a future occasion.

There is one high fall along Ladysmith Main; a hundred yards long and forty feet high in one place; that means at least 1,000 tons to be filled [??] away.

In one 'heading' we found twelve men in a group; they had missed the blast, had gathered together, and been killed by afterdamp (carbon monoxide). And what a spectacle! A dead horse lay rotting near by, and the men had fallen in all shapes, some had sat and died in a heap, some stretched on their backs, six were lying across one another; mortification had played havoc, faces and bare arms white with mildew. The nauseating stench adding to the horror of it all. In other places the poor fellows had been killed mercifully quickly at work, stooping cutting coal, their tools fallen by them. One on the 'main' had his clothes burnt right off his. One man was on his knee by a full tram of coal, chalking his number. The blast in one place had blown a horse and tram against the coal face, pinning a father and son against the coal. A sickening sight. The awful tragedy of it all; the criminal negligence involved. And the Coal Mines Regulation Acts were passed in 1872, forty years ago, and amended times since; and these preventable holocausts still occur.

The Stooped Urn, filling, dips and flashes:
The bronzed brims are deep in ashes;

The pale old lips of Death are fed;
Shall this Dust gather flesh hereafter?
Shall one shed tears, or fall to laughter,
At sight of all these poor old Dead?

Then the 'Dead March', what a nightmare. We draw on leather gloves, lift a body onto a sheet of brattice cloth, wrap it up, then tie it on a stretcher. 'Off with it, boys', and what a journey, even to us, used to pit work. Through the murky gloom. Dimly lit by the swinging lamps carried by the bearers, broken timbers overhead, cracking with the continual squeeze; stumbling over the rough road with the swaying burdens, slipping on rails, sleepers, rough stones, stepping over small falls; timber, here and there the carcass of a horse stretched across the road, bursted and mortifying. Climbing big falls. Squeezing through small, hastily prepared passages, great stones hanging overhead, likely to fall at any minute. One did fall and broke a stretcher. And the stupefying heat and bad air, causing the sweat to pour down one in streams, and to add to the romance the sickening stench, rising all the time, to the face of the man behind. In one place, wading to our knees in water; one man fell with the stretcher. Some bodies are heavy too, our wrists giving out before the two miles are covered. Now the pit bottom is reached and the cold air chills to the bone.

In the carriage with the burden; the hitcher pressed the button, up we go, half a mile of shaft in less than a minute, a rushing and settling. Then across the colliery yard, lit by electricity, through groups of men and women, 'Who is it?' 'Don't know, indeed', on we go. To the mortuary, walls piled with coffins; men come forward, noses and mouths covered; unwrap the body, calling out to a man with a book. 'Moleskin trousers, patch on left knee, nailed boots, piece on right heel' etc, etc, usually the only means of identification, as faces are unrecognisable. Twenty have so far been buried unidentified, owing to melting. Funerals take place every day, the sad processions slowly winding their way to the hillside cemetery.

The pity of it all, that flesh should be so cheap!

The 20th Century. The Age of Luxury! The Triumph of Wealth

Production! Of Labour-Saving and Life-Saving Appliances and 450 of the highest evolved species of animal needlessly sacrificed!!

Everyone in connection with mining, and anyone outside who reads at all knows that accumulation of gas can be prevented by efficient ventilation; that dusty roads can be avoided by regular waterings. Why the Hell are these things neglected? Because of the expense! And labour being so dirt cheap. Look you! The average L.M.Coll. Co. turns over its invested capital every eight years; and the Capitalists' blood-stained claw still reaches for more.

I don't expect the Manager of the Colliery, the Mines Agent for District, together with the Managing Director of Col. Co., Lord Merthyr, will be re arraigned for manslaughter; by suffering Christ, they should be! I don't know if I shall stay through the Exploring. I am fed up. Emily, always prejudiced against pit-work, is ten times so now. I like this locality, too. We live in a beautifully wooded district, just outside the old town of Caerphilly, four miles from Senghenydd, training to work, nights 9–3. I walk back, down a lovely valley. I have been fairly well satisfied here too; £2. 1s for a 48-hour week, and not too much work. From our doorstep we can see fields and lanes and woods, and little solitary dingles running between the mountains. Such walks, such a wealth of treasure to a nature-lover. The days this grand summer that I have lain with a book in the shadow of the old mediaeval castle. Yes, I like this place better than any before.

Am pleased to hear of the success of the M.E. Union; all industries are grouping now, and labour is beginning to understand. Look at New Zealand. The Enginemen's Stokers' and Surface Craftsmen's Union has decided to merge with the S.W. Miners' Federation. Of course the Capitalist Octopus is not afraid of petty little Labour MPs but it shudders at the "New Labour Movement".

We four are well, the baby, Syd, is a young uncompromising rebel of two years. The girl, Kate a little philosopher of three and a half. I trust you and yours are well. If I come to Birmingham at Christmas, or before, I will let you know.

I remain your sincere cousin
(Signed) Will Fisher

In Memoriam

*Captions to photographs sent by Ceri Thompson,
Curator, Big Pit, Blaenafon*

Charred pit prop
*'... and all the timber, so far as I could
see from there on was all ablaze ...' Mr
Shaw, the colliery manager, quoted in
the Home Office Report. This piece of
badly charred timber support was
recovered after the disaster, having
been found near the body of Samuel
Booth of 43 Edward Terrace,
Abertridwr. Apparently Samuel's
father was also working down
Senghenydd that day but survived.*

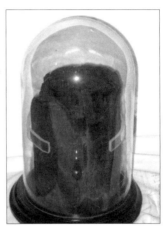

Draeger Breathing Apparatus
*In 2003 a German-designed
Draeger breathing apparatus was
donated to the museum by Dinas
Mines Rescue Station. This type of
apparatus was introduced into
service around 1904 and used in a
number of mining disasters in
Europe and the USA. They were so
popular that United States mine
rescue workers became known as
'Draeger men'. The museum's
example appears to be the 1908/09
model and was probably used
during the Senghenydd disaster as
this is the design worn by rescue
men during the rescue attempts. In*

spite of the success of the Draeger it was replaced by the British made Proto apparatus during the run-up to the first world war.

Presentation pocket watch
Gold pocket watch presented to Mr Charles Adams by Llanhilleth Colliery officials and friends in recognition of his services rendered at the Senghenydd explosion October 1913.

Flame safety lamp
According to the Home Office report that the safety lamp used at the Universal Colliery in 1913 was the Cambrian type made by Thomas and Williams of Aberdare. Lamps were lit, locked and issued to workmen and officials in the surface lamproom. They were again examined underground at the beginning of a shift in places known as 'locking stations'. If a lamp became extinguished underground a man had to go to a 'lamp cabin' where men known as 'lamp lockers' would re-light it. An open light in

the West side lamp cabin was put forward as a possible cause of the explosion.

There were hundreds of Cambrian lamps underground on 14 October in 1913 but none have been donated to the National Museum. However a lamp associated with the disaster is in the collection: this is a Hepple-white Gray flame safety lamp owned by Mr Bowen Jones of 4 Philips Terrace, Senghenydd. The details given to the museum were sketchy but it appears that the lamp was given to Mr Jones's workmate Bill Wedlock, whose family kept it until it was donated to the museum.

The Hepplewhite Gray lamp was usually used by mine officials rather than workmen (although their use is not mentioned as being the practice at the Universal Colliery in 1913) and it it is possible that Mr Bowen Jones was one of them, although his name doesn't appear as one of the fourteen 'firemen' down the pit at the time of the explosion.

Tobacco tin
This tobacco (or 'twist') container is engraved 'Gabe Wigley, 59 High Street, Senghenydd, 1913'. Unfortunately the donor didn't have details of who Mr Wigley was.

Commemorative plate
Hand-painted plate, 'In loving memory of my dear brother Phillip Lower aged 22 years who was accidently killed in Senghenydd explosion Oct. 14 1913. A sudden change and in a moment fell I had not time to bid my friends farewell. Think this not strange death happens unto all. This day was mine tomorrow you may

fall. He's gone to rest.'
Phillip Lower lived in 17 St
Cenydd Terrace,
Senghenydd.

Pocket watch

The task of identifying hundreds of bodies, often badly burnt or otherwise mutilated, was very difficult. Men and boys had often to be identified by clothing or personal possessions. William Edward Beck came to south Wales from Broadway in Somerset to look for work sometime before 1900. Mr Beck's body could be identified only by this watch. A dent in the back was caused either by the explosion or by a fall of ground caused by a burning roof support. He was forty-three years old when he died and lived at 45 Springfield Terrace, Nelson. He was apparently found near to his cousin and both are now buried in Ystrad Mynach churchyard.

More press reports

The Liverpool Daily Post and Mercury
Wednesday 15 October 1913

AWFUL PIT DISASTER
EXPLOSION AND FIRE
445 MEN ENTOMBED
LITTLE HOPE OF ESCAPE
BRAVE RESCUE WORK
ROYAL MESSAGE OF SYMPATHY

A disastrous explosion, which threatens to be the most appalling in the history of the Welsh coalfield, took place yesterday morning at the Universal Pit, Senghenydd, near Cardiff. The total number of men and boys in the mine was 931. The eastern section seems to have been affected very slightly, the men there being rescued. All those in the western or Lancaster Section, it is feared, have fallen victims of the explosion and its consequent fire. The flames gained ground despite all the brave efforts of the rescue parties, who were cut off from that portion of the workings where their comrades lay. Eleven bodies have been recovered, and 434 persons have yet to be accounted for.

When the explosion took place the pithead gear was practically destroyed, and the banksman, named Moggridge, had his head blown from his body. The neighbourhood was shaken by the report, and in a very short time there were large crowds of men, women and children at the pithead, anxiously making inquiries.

Sad sights were witnessed around the colliery. Aged women and young girls were bemoaning together the absence of news of their beloved ones, and here and there strong men and women fell upon the neck of those dear to them as they came up from the depths below.

A remarkable circumstance is that a similar disaster occurred in this pit in May 1901, when more than eighty lives were lost, only one man escaping.

King George has sent a message expressing the deep sorrow with which he and the Queen heard yesterday's news.

Survivors' stories

LITTLE BOY'S FIRST EXPERIENCE

Sydney Gregory, of Station Terrace, Senghenydd, who was working at the Lancaster Pit, said:

> It was somewhere about eight o'clock when I heard two heavy thuds. Then there were clouds of smoke. The air suddenly became still, and this was followed by coal dust as thick as fog. I could hardly see my way about. A little boy from Aber, who started work as a colliery lad this morning, was with me, and he began to cry, and asked me what was the matter. I told him it would be all right. A man arrived and persuaded us to go out. As we were proceeding we could hear the fires raging. It was awful. Timber was cracking and falling about, and we could hardly stand the heat and foul air. At last we got to the bottom of the pit, and remained there nearly two hours. There were a lot of colliers there, and they hardly seemed to know what had happened. The little boy was crying, and I gave him some water. He then got all right. Shortly after ten o'clock we were taken to the surface.

A GRIM PROCESSION

At night, as darkness settled over the Valley, whose slopes were illuminated with the countless lights from the colliers' cottages, a grim procession of undertakers with coffins wended its way to the pithead, and the dead were encased and removed to their homes, from which they had gone out in the early hours of the morning full of strength and vigour.

In an interview, last evening, with a squad of men from the

Rhymney Valley rescue brigade, as they emerged from the pit with oxygen apparatus over their shoulders, they expressed their regret that so far they had not been able to bring out anyone alive. They said they had gone down in sections of the fire throughout the day, and had been working on the flames. They had made good progress, but they confessed that it was hopeless to try to reach the entombed men until the fire was extinguished. They had played a hose on the flames, and had used hundreds of extinguishers with considerable effect.

As showing the uncertain nature of a miner's work, it is interesting to record that some of the colliers who were hewing at the coal-face in the distant parts of the unaffected York Pit continued operations until 9.30, an hour and a half after the explosion happened, being wholly oblivious of the tragedy enacted at the other end of the mine.

Although there is a galaxy of expert mining engineers at the

One of the funerals, with huge crowds paying homage

colliery, no one will venture an opinion as to the cause of the explosion, which can be ascertained only after careful investigation by Mr Redmayne and his staff.

The County Times (Pembrokeshire)
16 October 1913

COLLIERY EXPLOSION
Overwhelming Calamity at Senghenydd
480 Men Entombed
Scenes of Horror

The annals of disaster in the coalfields of South Wales and Monmouthshire provide no parallel in circumstances of horror and doom to the overwhelming clamity which overtook the mining village of Senghenydd on Tuesday morning.

At 6 o'clock 921 workmen employed by the Lewis Merthyr Consolidated Collieries Company descended the shaft for the day's work. At 8 o'clock there was a thunderous explosion in the western section of the Lancaster Pit, and its reverberating roar travelled through all the colliery workings, extending into the York Pit districts of the same colliery undertaking, a long way distance from the immediate theatre of the blast. So severe was the explosion that the pit banksman, John Moggridge, was blown yards away from the spot where he was engaged, and killed instantly.

The roar of the blast brought the villagers – many of whom had not long awakened from their night slumber – hurrying to the scene, whilst mine rescue teams resident in the neighbourhood were promptly called to the aid of the entombed men.

Colliery officials and doctors were also prompt to answer the appeal for assistance, the magic signification and potential horror of the call evoking that eager competition for service and sacrifice which has so recent a parallel in the marine race of ocean greyhounds to the burning liner in mid-Atlantic immediately the S.O.S. message winged its way over the deep sea.

A minister tries to help

The County Times (Pembrokeshire)
23 October 1913

100,000 Visitors at Senghenydd on Sunday

Last Sunday was characterised by scenes of extraordinary animation at Senghenydd.

As early as eight o'clock in the morning hundreds of curious sightseers had poured into the little township from the adjoining valleys, and the mountains, which stand silent sentinels over the scene, were literally black with processions of men and women.

As the day wore on trains, motor cars, motor cycles and other conveyances brought thousands more to the scene, and the main road leading to Caerphilly was almost impassable. The entrances to the colliery were thronged with people, and here and there amid the crowds stood little knots of men and women whose pallid, anxious faces betokened something more than sympathetic curiosity. It is estimated that over 100,000 people visited the colliery during the day.

The ordinary services at the churches were suspended, the sermon had perforce to give way to prayer meetings, which were attended in the main by very small congregations. At one place of worship the congregation barely mustered two dozen, the majority being grey-haired, many scattered veterans of the mine, who knew full well the horror of all that had happened since their last meeting together.

A mass for the dead was celebrated at Cwm Aber School, Abertridwr, by the congregation of Roman Catholics. Of this small community thirty-two have been brought up dead, or are among those who are still in the sealed grave below. Father Knight, who officiated, asked those present to pray for the repose of the souls already passed away, and added that a similar service was being held in all the Roman Catholic churches throughout the district.

At Salem (Welsh Baptist) Chapel, the service was of a particularly moving character. Of this church twelve or more have perished in the fatal blast, and the supplications were mingled with choking sobs. The pastor, the Rev David Roberts, who was the foreman of the jury at the inquest on the victims of the last disaster, spoke in moving tones of the terrible fate which had befallen so many of their neighbours.

The wider impact

The explosion on 14 October 1913 was not just a disaster for Senghenydd and that area. The reverberations carried right across Wales – and further. Local papers carried heartbreaking stories. It is interesting that some papers reported in full, many times, and with great feeling, when some seemed almost to be unaware of the disaster.

The Pembrokeshire *County Times* of 16 October reported that Mrs Davies from Coldstone, Little Newcastle, had had three sons in the mine – one was alive, one dead, one missing. The same paper, on 23 October, said that Thomas Mendus from Dyffryn, Dinas Cross (between Newport and Fishguard) was lost: 'At the time of writing no trace has been found of him'.

The *Cambrian News* (17 October) carried an interview with Rev. Evan Thomas, pastor of the Tabernacle Calvinistic Methodist church, Senghenydd. He told of:

> the three brothers Hughes, who came here from Ffestiniog last August. Three fine young men! ... Hugh Parry, who lodged at Commercial Street, came from Porthmadog, and was superintendent of my children's Sunday School. Idrisyn Hymphreys, a native of Abergynolwyn, was another faithful member. He was a fine tenor singer and always ready to assist in our meetings and councils.

A later issue of the paper mentions that Hugh, the eldest of the three Hughes brothers, was twenty-five. The three brothers left eight children, one a baby aged eighteen months.

William Owen Williams, from the same town, also died; however, Evan Jones and his son Owen Jones had lain down together to die, but were found by rescuers just in time.

According to *Yr Herald Cymraeg* (21 October 1913), Idrisyn Humphreys was also an expert on the tenor harp. He had moved to the south about four years before the disaster, 'when work came to an end in Bryn Eglwys'.

One chapel in Senghenydd lost three-fifths of its male members.

The *Montgomeryshire Express* and *Radnor Times* was clearly affected by the long list of local men who had died. Llanidloes, with its townsmen all around the south Wales coalfield, lost several in Senghenydd: Thomas Meredith, Richard Rees, Thomas Morgan and George Edwards. One of the rescuers was also from Llanidloes: Mr J. M. Kitto, superintendent of the Rhymney Reserve Brigade. Thomas Meredith from Newtown, well-known and much liked in the town, was one who died. In Welshpool, they mourned James Thomas and William George Davies. George Davies had adopted a relative's son, John Davies, then aged seventeen, who was rescued. Several natives of Machynlleth were working at Senghenydd, but all were found to be safe; however, one local man died: William Jones from the tiny village of Aberangell. Mrs Norton of Dolcorsllwyn Hall, Cemmaes, reported that two of her former servants were among the victims. William Griffiths from Dolanog, near Llanfair, was killed, and Kerry's policeman, PC Hopkins, had a brother still entombed in the pit, and Mr Edwin Stephens' son and son-in-law had died. Llanfyllin's Jack Evans was reported safe, but Thomas Jones was missing.

Further north still, men were being mourned, or worried about. The *Caernarvon and Denbigh Herald*, on 24 October, carried news of many local men. On 17 October, it seemed likely that only one man from the area had been in the pit at the time. This was 19-year-old William Abel Jones of Colwyn Bay. His father was a 'much-esteemed postman'. A few weeks before, Abel had decided to try his luck at coal-mining, induced down to Senghenydd by a friend (who had been on the night shift and was therefore not in the pit at the time of the explosion). Abel's father went down to Senghenydd as soon as he heard about the disaster, and sent a telegram to his wife saying that he had no news ... Sadly, Abel's name later appeared on the list of the dead.

The later issue of the paper mentions the 'three fine men' mentioned by Rev. Evan Thomas, William, Hugh and Humphrey Hughes, from Blaenau Ffestiniog. They had gone down to Senghenydd only three months before. Hugh, the eldest, was twenty-five. William Owen Williams, from the same town, also died; however, Evan Jones and his son Owen Jones were found by rescuers, just in time.

Three Caernarfon men died: Richard Thomas, and brothers Thomas and Richard Fearne.

The small village of Trawsfynydd was particularly cruelly hit. Ten of its young men were killed: William Williams, John and Meurig Morris, three Evans brothers, John Griffith, Willie Jones, Evan and Edmund Roberts. Two others, John and William Jones, were. rescued and reported detained at a Cardiff hospital.

Bethesda lost two brothers, George and Ellis Davies, and also William Williams. Richard Jones of Penygroes was rescued; nothing was known of his son, Richard Owen Jones, or of another man from the village, Mr Jones. Local men also missing at the time of the newspaper report were Hugh Parry and Hugh Jones.

But on searching the 1911 Census for the names of those killed it is clear that many came from England, and some from Ireland. Henry Brooks, for example, was from Biggleswade. Brothers Bertie and Harold Button came from 'Summersetshire', as did Henry William Ford. Francis Clarke and Edward Gilbert were from Devon. Stanford Hezekiah Dando was from Coalpit Heath, in Gloucestershire – the Census says he was a police constable in 1911. King Samuel Humphries was from Charfield in Gloucestershire; he left his wife, Mary, and four sons and three daughters. Lewis Musty had come from Bristol; he and his son-in-law Henry Davies, also born in Bristol, both died. Herbert Delbridge has a Cornish name; Charles Emery had been a builder's labourer in North Wooton, Somerset, in

1911. Another from Bristol was William Joseph Hyatt – he left a wife, five sons and four daughters. John Richard Kirkham was the son of a miner; in 1911 John was a tailor's clerk in Tipton. James Lower was from Curry Rivel, Somerset. Richard Newell was from Bath, Albert Pegler from Stroud, Harry Penny from Yeovil. George Bastyn and Walter Berry – two young men around the same age – were they friends? Cousins, perhaps? – had travelled from the small village of Ottery St Mary in Devon to work in the pit.

Some of the Irishmen were Peter Carr (Cork); James Druhan (New Ross); Joseph Hopkins (Kerry); James Stephens (Kerry); Patrick Sullivan could also have been Irish.

A postcard home to Trawsfynydd

In an antiques fair in 2011, John Roberts of Abertridwr bought an old postcard, showing a picture of the Welsh Methodist Chapel, Senghenydd. The message on the back is in Welsh, and in a few short lines, squeezed into the space headed 'This space for correspondence', captures all the fear, grief and sadness that resulted from the explosion at the Universal Colliery.

The card is addressed to 'Mrs I. [or J.] Roberts, No. 5 Ardudwy, Station Road, Trawsfynydd, North Wales' and is date-stamped 3.15 p.m., 15th October 1913, the day after the disaster:

> Dear Parents, Just a couple of words hoping that you are both well up there. I expect you've heard about the explosion in Senghenydd. I've been here since yesterday. They haven't found Jack Davies yet. There are hundreds they can't get to. Will and Jack Tynllyn were brought up safely

No. 5 Ardudwy Street as it is today

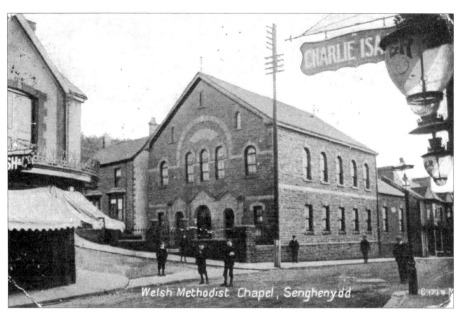

The postcard

this morning. There are lots from here still down there. I'll send details later. Yours, Bob

Above the words '*This space for correspondence,*' this message has been added:

Ann Jones's sons were killed. Edmwnd for certain, and possibly Evan too.

Jac Ty'n Llyn's family

In 2012 Rhianydd Jones, a resident of Plas Cwm Parc flats for the elderly in Senghenydd, gave the following account of the disaster to the Reverend Denzil John, Caerphilly. She told him that two of her relations, Will and Jac, were caught up in the explosion. They were the very last men to be brought from the shaft alive. The last survivors, eighteen in all, were rescued from the Bottanic District in the early hours of 15 October. On the official list the two men are named as:

6. John (Jac) Owen Jones, 183 Caerphilly Road, Senghenydd
17. William Jones, 65 Hugh Street, Senghenydd

These are the very same Will and Jack Tynllyn who are

Jac Ty'n Llyn with his son, John Francis, about 1923

mentioned on the postcard. According to Rhianydd Jones, Jac had refused to move until the rescue team found his brother and brought him to safety. John Roberts, the new owner of the postcard, took it to show her.

Jac Ty'n Llyn, Trawsfynydd, was my father-in-law. He was cousin to Hedd Wyn. I married his son, John Francis Jones, who was born in 1920. In the long hours they'd spent underground

Ty'n Llyn today

Daniel Davies in the Great War   *Rhianydd Jones during the Second World War*

John Roberts, Abertridwr

waiting to be rescued, the gas had got to Will and Jac. They couldn't work underground after that. Will went to Cardiff to do light work in a factory. Jac worked on the railway in Senghenydd, and lived in Bryn Hyfryd.

My mother was from Senghenydd, but my father came from Dihewyd, near Aberaeron. His name was Daniel Davies, and he not only insisted on handing on the Welsh language but also made sure that I spoke the Ceredigion dialect! He would take me into the front room on Sunday afternoons and teach me to recite the psalms and bits of poetry. I still remember them. Farms were in a bad way at the beginning of the last century, and that's why he came to the Universal Colliery. He was working the night before the fire and came up from the pit at six o'clock in the morning. The amazing thing is that many of those who survived the accident were in the Great War after that – including my Dad, Wil and Jac.

My schoolfriend's grandfather was not so lucky. Enid Jones was an assistant in the men's clothes shop in Senghenydd, and her grandfather was killed on the morning of the explosion. They didn't find his body for a month, and only recognised him by a watch he'd been given as a present. It was in his coat pocket and had stopped at twenty-five past eight.

Rhianydd, the eldest of the five Bryn Hyfryd children

76

Part of Caerphilly Road, where Jac Ty'n Llyn was a lodger

Ruin of the old home, Ty'n Llyn, Trawsfynydd, on the road to Yr Ysgwrn. The mil on Nant Pompren Hwch was there, and according to one Census, four families lived there.

The Traws boy – Jack Ty'n Llyn is one of the two on the pony

Jac, his wife, and their only son John Francis

John Francis, Rhianydd, and Jac and his wife

Convalescent home in Porthcawl, for some of the survivors of the disaster. Jac is front left.

Jac (front left) with fellow railway workers at his retirement party

A card from Jac showing he was in France, September 1915

Jac (front), Wil (right back) and two other brothers, in the Great War

Release Certificate for Jack leaving the army. Gas had affected his lungs, so he was listed as 'disabled'

The burial of the bodies

Last week the bodies of seven Trawsfynydd men were discovered in the pit in Senghenydd. They were buried on Friday, Saturday and Sunday last. Four are still unaccounted for, and it is feared that they will not be reached before Christmas. Our deepest sympathies go to the grieving families. The two Morris brothers were buried on Sunday.

Y Glorian, November 15 (1913), 5 col. 2

An old postcard of Trawsfynydd at the beginning of the twentieth century

A report on the losses of Trawsfynydd and district

To mark the seventieth anniversary of the explosion, the June 1983 issue of *Yr Herald Cymraeg* contained an article on the Bro Ffestiniog men who had lost their lives. It ended with this account of the Trawsfynydd victims. The two men, referred to as 'Ann Jones' sons' on the postcard, are mentioned in the third paragraph. The newspaper was sent in by Laura Williams, Pwllheli. Her father's father was John Thomas, Coed Rhygyn, father of six sons, who was lost in the first Senghenydd explosion, and is named in the first paragraph:

To conclude our story of Senghenydd, let us see how the disaster affected Trawsfynydd. Trawsfynydd had lost one of its men in the Senghenydd explosion at the beginning of the century. His name was John Thomas, Coed Rhygyn, and while researching this article, I was able to speak to his daughter, Annie Thomas, who still lives in Traws.

Ty Llwyd Terrace with the military camp on Bryngolau fields in the background

Castle House, Trawsfynydd, which was a shop at the beginning of the twentieth century

Castell today

Fronwnion, where Willie Jones was brought up, as it is today

Evan Jones's gravestone in Penyrheol cemetery

The two brothers from Trawsfynydd killed in Senghenydd in 1913 were John Morris and Meurig Morris, Ty Llwyd Terrace. Robert John Morris, son of John Morris, now lives in Llandegai. He was a child in 1913, and had already lost his mother, in 1912. I talked with Griffith Morris and Nellie Morris, nephew and niece of the two brothers, who live in Traws.

Two other brothers killed in 1913 were Evan and Edmund Jones, Castle House. It was reported that John Evans, Penrallt, lost three sons. John Evans does not appear to be a native of Trawsfynydd, and I couldn't find anyone who knew of the three brothers. John Evans was apparently from Dolwyddelan, and also lived in Blaenau Ffestiniog for a time. Richard, William and Robert were the names of the sons.

John Griffith Owen, Glascoed, was definitely from Trawsfynydd, and relatives of his still live there. Another who lost his life was William Williams, son of Hugh Williams, Tŷ Llwyd Terrace. Willie Jones, Fronwnion and Johnny Davies, Tynrhedyn, were also named.

The decline of the slate quarries at the start of the twentieth century

The Penrhyn Quarry produced 100,000 tons of finished slate per year in 1899. However, one of the effects of the Great Penrhyn Strike between 1900 and 1903 was a huge drop in production from the quarries of the old county of Caernarvonshire. As Dafydd Roberts said in his lecture *Y Chwarelwr a'r Sowth* (The Quarryman and the South) (Gwynedd County Council, 1982), far more foreign slate was imported into the British Isles during the first years of the twentieth century. There was also a significant drop in the number of houses built in Britain:

1900	139.7 thousand
1904	136.6 thousand

1908	100.9 thousand
1912	53.4 thousand

The blue slate had to compete more and more against clay roof tiles; exports of Gwynedd slate fell from 35,600 tons in 1900 to 24,500 tons in 1910.

By the second decade of the twentieth century, recession, unemployment and the lack of promising predictions for the future meant that there was a marked increase in migration from the quarrying areas.

Dafydd Roberts also offers another relevant fact which explains why many of the quarrymen moved to the coalmines in south Wales:

A quarryman on the face of an underground quarry in Blaenau Ffestiniog

The migration was facilitated by the Union of Quarrymen, which arranged for faithful Union men – and there were many of them – who had held a union card for some years, to transfer their membership directly to the Federation of South Wales' Miners (or the Fed, as it was called) without having to pay the membership deposit for that union. The strength of the flow to the south was added to because of the First World War. Due to their experience as stoneworkers, quarrymen would have no difficulty in being employed as coalminers ...

... [there was] a quite significant movement from the quarrying areas in Gwynedd to the south in the years before the First World War. There are numerous references in newspapers from the period, describing the tearful scenes at the railway stations in

A group of Blaenau Ffestiniog quarrymen at the end of the nineteenth century

Gwynedd on public holidays, the times when the emigrants could return to their impoverished families. A common scene in the dramas of the period was that on the platform with the wife farewelling with her husband who was setting out for the south to earn his crust.

Dafydd Roberts also raises the curtain on another custom – the tendency for quarrymen from one village/valley to move to the same mining valley in south Wales:

Listen to the experience of an old friend from Corris, who used to write to me, and who is now more than eighty years old. He started work in a coalmine in 1912, although he was brought up in Corris. He had to leave home as there was no work to be had in Corris and Aberllefenni. This is part of his story:

It was very rare for the word South to be used, and the

northerner was a Bloody Northman. It cannot be said that the 'Hwntw' (South Walian) and the 'Northman' were fond of each other. The Northman was used to living on a very small wage, and knew how to live frugally, whilst wages in the South were considerably better, although my first wage as a green collier was 12/- a week, and I remember my budget well – 3/- for mam, 3/- for lodgings, 4/6 for food and the 1/6 that was over for totally necessary things. Another factor that differentiated the Northerners and the Southerners is as they were in lodgings, there wasn't a warm welcome waiting for them at home in the evenings, so there would be groups along the road in each other's company, whilst the Southerners would be in their homes. The majority of those from Corris would always go to Bedlinog, so much so that it was called 'Corris Bach' (Little Corris); and another place was Penrhiwceibr, and a lot of the children were married there, some still maintaining a

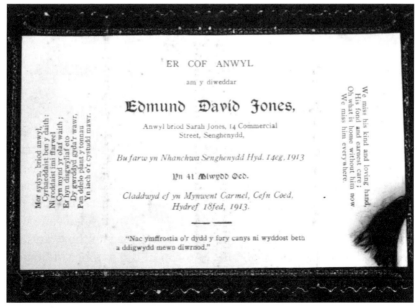

A memorial card for one who lost his life in the explosion:
'Edmwnd' is one of the Trawsfynydd boys mentioned on the
postcard

connection with Corris. The Northerners were more for the chapel (somewhere to go, perhaps) than the Southerners, and in the Sunday School I heard heated debates, the Southerners always bringing politics into the discussion, and insisting that Christ was a Socialist. Remember at the same time that the Northerners were Radical Liberals, bordering on Socialists ... I remember that a lot came home from the South to vote for Haydn Jones in Meirionnydd, many of them walking all the way ...'

There is material there in that quote for a series of lectures, I'm sure, but I would like to draw your attention especially to one part of that which was said, which is that the quarrymen of Corris and the area would go Bedlinog or Penrhiwceibr. This is extremely interesting, and there is some evidence that there was a tendency for people from different rural areas of Gwynedd to move to particular areas in the south – perhaps because friends, a brother or sister had gone there, starting a movement which snowballed.

The family of John and Jane Morris, Trawsfynydd

The Penrhyn Quarry produced 100,000 tons of finished slate per year in 1899. However, one of the effects of the Great Penrhyn Strike between 1900 and 1903 was a huge drop in production from the quarries of the old county of Caernarvonshire. As Dafydd Roberts said in his lecture *Y Chwarelwr a'r Sowth* (The Quarryman and the South) (Gwynedd County Council, 1982), far more foreign slate was imported into the British Isles during the first years of the twentieth century. There was also a significant drop in the number of houses built in Britain:

*In the middle of the back row are John and Meurig Morris,
the two sons who were killed in Senghenydd.
On the right of the picture are the two sons who emigrated to
America. Neli, mother of Jean Hughes, sits between her parents
in the front row.*

According to the records, at the time of the accident John Morris lived in 18 Brynhyfryd Terrace and Meurig Morris in 6 School Street, Senghenydd. John had married Sarah. Their first child died, and Sarah herself died at the birth of the second.

John Morris in 1912

At the family grave. John and Sarah's 13-month-old daughter Lizzie died in 1909. Sarah died when giving birth to their son Bob in 1912, and John lost his life in 1913

The grandparents with their orphan grandson Bob (Robert John), John's son. After his father's death, he was brought up in Trawsfynydd by his grandparents

Bob in old age at his parents' grave

Jean Hughes and her sons Hefin and Gareth remember the family at the graveside

The 1911 Census – workers from everywhere

The 1911 Census shows a large number of families and individuals from every part of Wales living or lodging in Senghenydd. The census form opposite for 8 Station Road, Senghenydd, is a typical example:

- The Head of the family, Evan Humphreys is originally from Ffestiniog, fifty-four years old and working on the coal picking belts in the colliery.
- His wife, Mary, is originally from Trefriw, in the Conway Valley and they have adopted a son from Bangor who is seven years old.
- There are three 'Boarders' lodging in the home: two from Trawsfynydd – Robert Morris who is an underground engine driver and Hugh Morris, who is a 'ripper' (removing waste stone) – and one from Swansea, Griffith Morgan, a land and mineral surveyor at the colliery.

By October 1913, there were two other colliers lodging at 8 Station Road – Lewis Misty and Samuel Curtis – and both are named on the lists of the dead.

Station Road, Senghennydd

CYFRIFIAD LLOEGR A CHYMRU, 1911.

Rhif Cyntaf.

Cyn ysgrifennu ar y Dasflen hon gweled yn dda dderbbyn yr Esiamplau a'r Cyfarwyddiadau a roddir ar y tu arall i'r papur, yn ogystal a phenawdau'r Colofnau. Dylid ysgrifennu mewn Inc.

Cewir cymmeyu y Dasflen yn gyfrinachol. Cymeryr gofal mwawaf na ddatguddir dim hysbysrwydd gysyfg a'r phersonnau unigol. Nid yw'r cyfrrofion i'w defnyddio i brof oed, megys mewn cysylltiad a Phensiynnau Henoed, nac i un pwrpas arall ond parottoi Tablau Ystadegol.

ENW A CHYFENW	TEBTYNAS I'R Pennaeth	OED a Rhyweliwyd a Rhyw.	MANYLION YNGLYN A PHRIODAS					GALWEDIGAETH NEU WAITH			Y LLE Y GANWYD	ANWYLDER	YR IAITH A LEFERIR
1	2	3	4	5	6	7	8	9	10	11	12	13	14
1 Evan Humphreys	Pennaeth	54	Priod					On Picking Belts of Scheme of Colliery	Gweithiwr		Merionydd Festiniog		Y ddwy
2 Mary Humphreys	Gwraig	53	Priod	32	4	1	3				Caernarfon Dolwen		Y ddwy
3 Percy Powell	Lletywr	4									Caernarfon Bangor		Y ddwy
4 Robert Morris	Brodist	28	Sengl					Engine Driver 3+9/10 underground in Colliery	Gweithiwr		Meirionydd Trawsfynydd		Y ddwy
5 Hugh Morris	Brodist	22	Sengl					Riper on Road Gravel in Coal Mine	Gweithiwr		Meirionydd Trawsfynydd		Y ddwy
6 Griffith Morgan	Brodist	32	Sengl					Landscape Mineral Surveyor	Gweithiwr		Morgannwg Pontardawe		Y ddwy
7													
8													
9													
10													
11													
12													
13													
14													
15													

(I'w lenwi gan y Cofrestrydd.)

	Gwryw.	Benyw.	Personau.
Cyfanswm			
	5	1	6

Yr wyf yn datgan fod y Dasflen hon wedi ei llenwi a'm gwybodaeth i a'm cred, yn gywir.

Arwydd: Evan Humphreys.

Cyfeiriad Post: 91 Station Road, Llwynypia, near Cardiff.

C. Reens

A letter from T. Meirion Griffiths

A miner from Trawsfynydd who was on the night shift

After reading your letter on the 1913 Senghenydd explosion in the June issue of *Llafar Bro*, I remembered hearing my uncle talk of the disaster. He was Evan Ellis Williams, my mother's brother, who died in March 1967 aged 95.

He left Llechwedd quarry and went down south at the beginning of the last century. He said that many local men went south at that time because you couldn't rely on wages from the quarry.

He worked nights on maintenance, making things ready for the colliers who started work at eight o'clock in the morning. He and his crew came up at eight o'clock on Monday morning October 14th, 1913.

It took him half an hour to walk home. On the way, he felt the ground tremble beneath his feet. He looked at his watch. It was exactly 8.20. He turned and ran back to the pit, and saw smoke coming from the shaft. There had been an explosion, and there was nothing anyone could do but wait for the rescue team to arrive and for the smoke and dust to clear.

Evan Elis Williams back home in Trawsfynydd

Soon hundreds of people had arrived at the pit. They were in shock and many were weeping for their loved ones in the depths below. It was a sad and terrible place. Only a few were rescued and 439 died. When it was safe for the men to go down, their job was to carry the bodies to the bottom

Evan Elis Williams with his great-grandson and great-granddaughter

of the shaft and bring them out of the pit into the fresh air. It took four or five men to bring one body out, and they could only manage two in one shift. Even that was too much for some. There were many who could only go down once a day.

It took them over three months to clear the site, and bring out the dead horses as well. It was absolutely dreadful.

My uncle was hale and hearty, and went on working there till his wife died in 1929. Then he came back north and went to work on farms as he had done when he was young.

He was a pacifist and a loyal chapel member, being a deacon and a Sunday School teacher.

One thing that infuriated him was the sight of the vicar encouraging young men to join up at the start of the First World War. 'Don't you think there's been enough loss of life here already?' he said to him. 'When *you* join the army, we'll be glad to see the back of you.' A fight would have broken out between them there and then, if the vicar hadn't left in some haste.

Yours,

T. Meirion Griffiths
Tyddyn Felin, Trawsfynydd

Meirion remembered his uncle describing the bad feeling between the Welsh and English miners underground. According to Evan some English miners were very cruel to the ponies. The Welsh and the Irish, on the other hand, were firm friends. No one dared start a punch-up in the pit itself. Any miner who did so would be given his cards immediately. Once above ground there'd be men who'd come looking for you. At such times it was a great comfort to have the Irish miners on your side!

The Senghenydd Explosion

Verses by Evan Williams
kept safely by
T. Meirion Griffiths

After reading your letter on the 1913 Senghenydd explosion in the June issue of *Llafar Bro*, I remembered hearing my uncle talk of the disaster. He was Evan Ellis Williams, my mother's brother, who died in March 1967 aged 95.

Canais ychydig y llynedd
Ar fore Nadolig gwyn,
Eleni mae pryder yn llanw'm bron
A phawb o'm deulu yn syn;
Daeth angau i Senghenydd
Yn arwr â'i gledd yn ei law
Gan ladd dros bedwar cant o wŷr –
Mae'r pentref oll mewn braw.

I sang a little last year
On a white Christmas morning,
This year worry fills my heart
And my family are all aghast;
Death came to Senghtnydd
A hero with sword in his hand
To kill over four hundred men –
The whole village in shock.

Ugeiniau o blant amddifad
A wnaeth mewn eiliad heb dad,
Gweddwon a mamau, tyrfa fawr,
A wylant trwy gyrau'r wlad;
Pedwerydd ar ddeg o Hydref
A gofiant trwy eu hoes,
Gwager y copwrdd ar aelwyd lom
I'w teimlad fydd yn loes.

Dozens of orphaned children
In a second left without a father,
Widows and mothers, a great crowd,
Weeping in all corners of the land;
The fourteenth of October
They will remember all their lives,
The empty cupboard in the bleak home
Will add an ache to their loss.

Welsh	English
Gwelais olion y danchwa	I was the remains of the explosion
Mewn difrod yn y gwaith,	In the devastation at work,
Darlunio allan fel yr oedd	Portraying it as it was
Mewn geiriau ni eill iaith;	In words no language could'
Mae deddfau Duw mor gyfrin	The laws of God are so cryptic
Yng nghyswllt tân a nwy	When it comes to fire and gas
Pan ddelant fin fin ffrwydro maent,	When they come together they explode,
Does gariad gan y ddwy.	There is no love in either.
Yn ebyrth i'r ddwy elfen frochus	A sacrifice to the two fuming elements
Tra'n ddiwyd gyda'u gwaith	Whilst diligent in their work
Rhai a yswyd gan angherdd tân	Some were consumed by the arduous fire
Eraill gan nwyon llaith;	Others by the damp gases;
Tyrfa tan gwympiadau	A crowd beneath falls
Wrth geisio dod i'r lan,	As they tried to reach the shore,
Ond marw pawb o bob gradd ac oed,	But all dead of every level and age,
Y nerthol fel y gwan.	The strong as well as the weak.
Gwelais gelanedd y meirwon	I saw the corpses of the dead
Fel oeddynt cyn y brad,	As they were before the betrayal,
Aml i fachgenyn llon ei fron	Many a boy with happy heart
Yn dynn wrth ochr ei dad;	Close to his father's side;
Ni wn beth oedd eu meddwl	I don't know what they thought
Ar riniog arall fyd,	On the threshold of another world,
Ochenaid drom gan rai at Dduw,	A deep sigh from some to God,
Eraill i'w cartref clyd.	Others to their happy home.
Mae llu o'n hen gyfeillion	A host of our old friends
Fu'n troedio yr hen fro	Who walked the old land
Yn gorwedd heddyw hyd y ẁys	Lie today along the track
Mewn heddwch yn y gro;	In peace in the grave;
Claddfa fel gardd o flodau	The cemetery like a flower garden
Welir ar bob llaw	To be seen on every side
Eraill yng ngwaelod y gwaith ar goll	Others at the bottom of the pit lost
A'u teulu'n ddwys gan fraw.	And their family engulfed in shock.

Carcharor yw'r tân heddyw	The fire today is a prisoner
Fel brenin y coed yn ei ffau,	Like the king of the wood in his lair,
Gwregys o dywod glan y môr	A belt of seaside sand
Yn gwylio'n hynod glau;	Watching ever so ready;
Pa hyd y deil ei oddaeth	For how long will he hold his fire
Ni wn, – pe delai'n rhydd	I don't know, – if he was set free
Gwna ddinystr eto fel o'r blaen,	He would destroy again as before,
Yn erchyll fyddo'r dydd.	Horrific the day if it comes.

Evan Williams's family remembers

This is the story of another Trawsfynydd family who lived in Senghenydd at the time of the explosion. The notes were compiled by Enid Roberts (Bangor) and Elfed Idris Williams (Yr Hendy).

The Family
Evan Williams (my grandfather, my father's father): Evan Williams was a native of Trawsfynydd
Mary Elen Welch (his wife): she was born in Chorlton-cum-Hardy (near Manchester). Her father was of Irish extraction, but her mother had roots in 'Brynffynnon', Trawsfynydd. After they married, they lived in Minffordd, Gwyndy, Trawsfynydd, before building Meirionfa. They had two sons and a daughter – William, Margaret Catherine and Emrys

Annie (Welch) Roberts: widow of George Welch – she then married Morris Roberts, Trawsfynydd (great-grandfather of Rhodri Glyn Thomas AM)

A relative?, William, his son (also in the pit at the time of the explosion) and Emrys, another son

Mary Elen (his wife), Annie (Welch) Roberts (his mother-in-law) and Evan Williams in Senghenydd

162 Commercial Street. Another branch of the family lived in Brynhyfryd Terrace (see right)

Annie* (Welch) Roberts, Margaret and William Jones (daughter and son-in-law), Annie May (daughter), a neighbour (?), Emrys* (cousin), Omri (son), William (son), Trefor (son). (* lived in 162 Commercial Street)

The move south

In 1912, like many others from the Trawsfynydd area, Evan Williams went to Senghenydd and found work in the Universal Pit. He was followed in May 1913 by his wife and children as well as other family members and friends. Evan and his family settled in 162 Commercial Street, Senghenydd.

Shortly before the explosion, Evan Williams asked the overseer of the Universal Pit if he and his son William could move from the 'small coal side' to the 'big coal side' (where the pay was much better, no doubt). Luckily for them, though they didn't realise it at the time, the request was refused. The explosion occurred on the 'big coal side' and both men were saved.

Nearly three-quarters of the miners lived in Senghenydd. The lives of the Welsh-speakers revolved around the church, the chapels, the school and the Eisteddfod.

Emrys was a pupil of Senghenydd School.
His first duty each morning, as soon as he reached school,
was to go down to the well and bring back a jugful of cold water
for the headmaster's whisky!

Evan Williams and his family were members of Tabernacl Chapel, where Margaret Catherine married Evan Thomas (Pentrefoelas) who also worked at the Universal Pit.

In 1920 Evan and Mary's adopted daughter, Laura, died of tuberculosis in Senghenydd. Mary Elen became very homesick and in 1921 returned to the north and bought Cae Du farm, Manod, Blaenau Ffestiniog.

Evan, and later Emrys, were both made deacons of Gwylfa CM Chapel, Manod. Emrys was a member of Blaenau Town Council and an official of the North Wales Quarrymen's Union, and later the TGWU, until his retirement at the end of the 60s.

It is not known which of the children wrote these verses, but they portray life in a coalminer's home.

Monday washday and its troubles
at 162 Commercial Street

This is a depressing day,
A busy day full of troubles,
A day which brings a heap of
Worry to Nain and me.
Evan bach is moaning
But there's no-one listening to him
The wash tub is on his mind,
Goodness me isn't it serious.

On the fire is a huge saucepan,
That's boiling its insides out,
As if it were saying authoritatively
It's washday today people.
Two old tubs on the kitchen floor
One of those quite fragile
In front of that Mag is scrubbing
Heaven help us it's time for you to finish.

Although I wait anxiously
To see the cosy kitchen
After finishing the wash
Here's another serious case.
Here's the woman filling the saucepan
Once again on the hearth
To go through the work
Which is a law to everyone in the house.

Soon a crew of 'blacks' come,
Mag scolding unable to stop,
Wil shouting 'Where's the drink?'
And the little shoes all over the place.
Em shouting about the tub
And the father looking for his pipe,
I turn my back quickly
Up to the bedroom to have a little nap.

A memorial card

Reports from Y Glorian, 1913

A visit to Senghenydd
by Mr Evan Williams, Porth

It was with pale features and a heavy heart that I directed my steps to this sad locality last Wednesday. The journey from Pontypridd took me over a bleak mountain, on a morning that was cold and wet with a heavy frost. As I went along I noted how swiftly 'human nature' becomes inured even to the sternest words of God. Last week, as I travelled this same road, the mountain was black with travellers, who were going as if 'to hear the Lord speak to them' through the disaster. Today I saw only a handful of haggard women, each with a loved one in that underground prison. On my way I met three brothers from Bl. Ffestiniog, Messrs. David Williams, Oak

Mount, Francis Hughes, Dorfil Street and Hugh Jones, Bowydd, F. H.'s friend. David Williams' son, and two of Francis Hughes' sons, are still missing. They had a look of hopelessness on their faces as they told me how bad things were that day. Out of 100 Rescuers only sixty-four had gone down the shaft, because of the polluted air. Of the twenty-four rescuers who went to one particular place, eighteen were overcome by fumes and had to be helped back to the surface.

When I reached Senghenydd, I realised, as I had on the mountainside, that the crowds had gone. Almost all the people at the pit head were friends and relatives, I believe, and the reader may well imagine their feelings after walking there many times a day for nine days, in the hope of seeing their loved ones released from their prison. But death still has them in its iron grasp. In my mind I heard the voices of those unfortunates saying to them, 'You are the ones who stayed with us in our s
uffering.' I met Messrs Evan Owen, Hugh Williams and his sons, John Morris, J. W.Jones, all from Trawsfynydd. They had relatives underground, and were weighed down by worry and grief. Despite every effort, all hope of seeing them brought out alive has disappeared, but they are keen to pay their last respects before leaving this doleful place, maybe for the last time.

The task of searching for the bodies goes on slowly but surely. The three great obstacles to their progress are Fire, Fumes, Falls. Reader, think of them having to bring out the bodies of three of their fellows one night, on top of about twenty-eight horses. Today the stench from the pit was horrifying. What can it be like at the bottom the shaft? It takes great courage to venture down. And yet the men do so willingly. They should be the subject of a heroic poem for some eisteddfod. It will be a long time before all the bodies are retrieved, and there may be some beneath the 'Falls' who will never be found. This is always the case after such a great disaster as this. I was told today that some of the foremost chapel men, of all denominations, lie at the bottom of the pit, and can just imagine how sad those places of worship must have been this past Sunday. There are said to be 250 widows and about 700 orphan children. The Lord Mayors of London, Cardiff, and other places have set up funds to assist them.

The heart of an entire nation has been touched, and money is flowing in. Theatres etc in this area are assisting, and collections will be made in all the chapels and churches of South Wales on Sunday next. I hope the North will also play its part. There are many North Walians here, and they will benefit from the Fund. Let us show that we can give as well as receive.

Y Glorian, November 1 (1913) 4 col 3-4

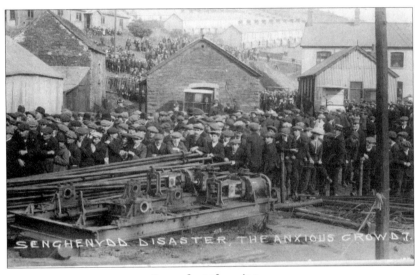

Crowd at the pit top

Notes from Trawsfynydd: the explosion in Senghenydd

Some of the people who went down to Senghenydd to identify their unfortunate relatives came home these past days, and their reports are most heartbreaking. How sad it was, they said, to see a cemetery with 150 open graves ready to receive the dead. The survivors are gaining strength, and have been shown every care and kindness. We were pleased to hear that the young man who suffered inflammation of the lungs is recovering well, and his mother is allowed to tend to him in the hospital. They expect many bodies to be brought out of the pit before the end of this week.

Y Glorian, November 1 (1913) 5 col 2

A visit to Senghenydd
the burial of many of the victims
(by Evan Williams, Porth, Rhondda)

How sad and sombre it was. I saw sights that I and the people of Senghenydd hope never to see again. The first sight that struck me was turning into the churchyard of Eglwysilan – a very ancient church, between Treforest and Senghenydd – and seeing thirty-six open graves waiting for their occupants and sorrow filled our hearts as we looked upon them, but a voice inside me said, 'Thou shalt see greater things than these.'

The grieving and the comforting

After we'd reached Abertridwr we met a funeral on its way to Penyrheol cemetery. Before it had gone from sight, another appeared, and another, the three like Job's messengers following close upon each other. The last of these was the funeral of W.H.Williams, from Trawsfynydd, and so I fell in behind it. After I'd reached the cemetery, another sight met my eyes. I'm told there were about 200 open graves, all sounding their message, 'Be thou prepared &c' and the words of Rev. E. Thomas (C.M.) on the fragility of human life were appropriate indeed, amidst the desperate outpouring that surrounded us on all sides.

On the way back we passed two more funerals heading for the same place, and when we reached Senghenydd a sombre and stately procession of five funerals was making its way to the same cemetery. One of them was the funeral of J. Davies, from Trawsfynydd, so I followed it. All along the way there were hundreds of people watching the procession. It was a sight I shall never forget. I cannot describe it. It would take the gifts of an angel to do so. I must leave it to the reader's imagination. 'History must be read and imagined.' One of the five dead men was a member of the Abertridwr Band. The Band played the Dead March, and Hymns, all along the way, and the sight of the man's instrument on top of his coffin brought tears to many an eye. I have heard some of the giants of the Welsh pulpit, of all denominations ... but this to me was the greatest sermon of all. ... Who knows how many fair hopes were yesterday laid in dust, how many bright futures were shrouded in darkness, how many shining stars were lost from their families' firmament. Many have groaned from the depths of their souls following this disaster, and only One can understand, only One can comfort. That is the story of Senghenydd.

On Friday there were fourteen funerals. I'm told there will be around twenty-five on Saturday. It is indeed a sorrowful melancholy place. On Saturday W. Jones (Fronwnion) and C. Morris, Cerryg y Drudion, were buried. They both lodged in Llanfabon with J.W.Jones of Trawsfynydd. On Sunday, J. and Meurig, the sons of John Morris, Trawsfynydd will be buried in the same place. I can but admire the dignity with which all the families have borne their misfortune. Losing your relatives so suddenly is a heavy and difficult cross to bear, but I think it is true to say that the feeling uppermost in their mind is gratitude for this opportunity of paying their last respects to their loved ones. During the past three weeks, they had lost all hope of seeing them again, so in the midst of their sorrow they are thankful for this great privilege. About 150 have been brought out so far, almost all of them in Ladysmith. Let us hope that those left in Kimberley and Pretoria will also be found. There is still great concern regarding them. On the whole it seems likely that they met their end without undue pain, as many have been easily identified and reclaimed. There are some exceptions. Despite the ferocity of the explosion only a few were buried without being identified. I was pleased to hear that the Free Church and Civic Councils were arranging a collection to help the widows etc.

Y Glorian, November 15 (1913) 2 Col 2-3

William Owen from Trawsfynydd remembers the seventy-fifth anniversary of the explosion

In 1988, the Avista company made a programme for S4C (n the series 'Dychryn') recounting the story of Senghenydd, produced by Owen Roberts and with John Bevan presenting. In the programme, William Owen from Trawsfynydd was interviewed. The poet Gwyn Thomas remembers him as 'Uncle Bill' – the family had moved from the north looking for work in the Universal coalmine.

William Owen was a young lad working in the pit in 1913. There were two lodgers staying at the family home – and they were also coalminers. Here are William Owen's words:

The two boys who were staying with us were not too fond of the chapel. We children had to go to the prayer meeting every Monday

The scene outside the mortuary at Senghenydd at the Universal Pit.

Funerals in Senghenydd

Welsh Pit Disaster. The Salvation Army Pitman's Funeral passing through Senghenydd.

night but the two of them went to the cinema that week. When they came home about eight o'clock that night, they were excited after seeing the film Four Dare Devils about trapeze artists in a circus. One had had an accident on the trapeze and had fallen to the arena, was wrapped in a

William Owen o Drawsfynydd

tarpaulin and carried from there. They took me as a guinea pig and wrapped me in a carpet and carried me on their shoulders saying: 'They'd do this if there was an explosion at the pit', laughing at the very idea.

The next morning, he had gone. He and his friend and had been blown to eternity ...

I was carrying the light that morning. I was at the pit about 7.30 in the morning and the fireman sent me to fetch the lights that were out and light them. I had to go down and when I was about 200 feet from the bottom of the pit I heard the bang. I didn't know what it was but after reaching the bottom, I saw that the doors had blown out and that there was a fire there. But I didn't understand that an explosion had happened. I walked some two miles underground to where the fireman was and told him what I had seen and heard, but the only thing he did was look at me in shock and tell me to go and work with Dic Richards for the rest of the day.

About 10.10, the fireman came to us and told us, 'Get out as soon as you can.' The fan which moved the air about the coalmine had turned off and that was the first sign that something was seriously wrong. Back we went at full pelt and by then the smoke was coming to meet us. The smell of the explosion, I suppose, was in our nostrils.

Up we went, and by then, there were thousands of people at the top of the pit waiting for news. That's when I understood that an explosion had happened but we didn't realise how may had been killed at the time ...

I met my Dad at the top of the pit. 'Go home to help your mum to prepare the beds in case they bring the lodgers up injured,' he said.

After having a bath and doing everything, I came back to the pit and I was underground again opening doors for the rescue teams. Fetch a bit of straw to make a bed for yourself, one of the men said. I did, but under the straw was the body of one of the coalminers, his eyes open and light.

I remember Mum and Dad had to go to the mortuary to try to identify the bodies of the two lodgers – they saw red thread on the socks of one and blue thread on the socks of the other, and that's how they identified them.

On the Friday after the explosion, I went down to Abertridwr to look for work in another mine.

The three brothers from Blaenau Ffestiniog

In Penyrheol cemetery near Senghenydd a slate gravestone bears the names of the three brothers from Blaenau Ffestiniog, William Griffith Hughes, aged twenty-three; Hugh Hughes, aged twenty-two; Humphrey Hughes, aged nineteen.

Searching for the story of the explosion in the Welsh newspapers for 1913, this quote from an eye-witness was seen in *Y Drych*, the American Welsh-language newspaper, 6 November 1913:

The Reverend Evan Thomas, minister of Tabernacle church, Senghenydd: 'Yes, the tragedy has hit the church very hard. The Noddfa Congregational Church lost two of its deacons – William

The Hughes brothers

Evans, 15 Coronation Terrace, Senghenydd, and Rees Evans, Caerphilly Road, Senghenydd. They have also lost very many of the best members of my own church down in the pit. Amongst them the three Hughes brothers, who came here from Ffestiniog last August. Three excellent young boys. Hugh Parry, who lodged at Commercial Street, came from Porthmadog, and he was a supervisor at the children's Sunday School; up until three weeks ago he worked in Aber. John H. Jones, Caerphilly Road, is another Northerner. He came from Ffestiniog. He was a faithful member of the church, leaving a widow and child. Another faithful member was Idris Wyn Hughes, from Abergynolwyn, near Towyn. He had a great tenor voice, and he would always be ready to serve in our meetings.

In June 2012 a letter to Llafar Bro, the Welsh-language newspaper for that area, brought a response from the family and local historians. The three brothers were the uncles of Emyr Hughes,

Blaenau Ffestiniog, and Gwenda Jones, Deganwy, who both contacted the editor after reading the letter. The brothers belonged to a family of twelve children, said Gwenda. Three more had died during childhood. Emyr had become interested in their story due to information uncovered by his aunt Mary Parry, Trefnant, who was the last of the fifteen children, and died in 2001. Another brother died in the Great War. He was killed on 30 April, 1918 at Esquelbecq. Llewelyn Hughes, Emyr's father, died as a result of an accident in Oakeley quarry in May 1960. The deaths in this family are typical of that generation, when many succumbed to childhood illnesses, coal, slate and war.

The body of William, the eldest son, was the first of the three to be brought out of the pit in Senghenydd. He was found on 16 October and buried on 19 October. It took another month to find the bodies of the two other brothers. They were found on 19 November and buried on 27 November. Their father spent three weeks in Senghenydd waiting for them to be brought out. According to Emyr, one son was identified by his distinctive shoes. Before they went away to work at the Universal, a shoemaker in New Road, Blaenau Ffestiniog, had made a special pair of shoes for all three. The other son was recognised by his watch, which was a reward for atttendance at Glan-y-Pwll school. Mel Goch from Llanffestiniog remembers hearing about them from his grandmother, who was their sister. According to his grandmother, one of the boys had swapped shifts, so that a lucky fellow-miner could take part in a rugby match.

William had worked in Kent before going down the mines. Some of his letters have been kept by his family. Later he went to work in Treherbert. In a letter dated 1911 he mentioned that his grandfather had died and that he hoped to have the old man's watch in memory of him. It's clear that all is not well at work:

All the men at the Pit where I'm working have gone on to the Jump. There's hardly anyone left here, and they've stopped all the lads apart from about half a dozen of us, and we don't know when we'll be stopped too.

A letter home, dated 1912, revealed that Wmffra (Humphrey) was down there with him. In the letter he mentioned the possibility of a day or two of strike action. In another letter from Treherbert, he wrote, 'I'm glad you've bought a house. I'll help you as much as I can.'

One letter survives from 9 Stanley Street, Senghenydd, where Wmffra was in lodgings. He promises to send money home 'next week' and claims that 'Griffith Evans is mistaken. I like it well enough here, and my health is improved. The people here say I'm getting fat, but I say I'm definitely turning grey.' He also promises to reply to 'Mag's' letter. He signs off saying it's time to attend the Band of Hope.

William was buried on the Sunday following the disaster. A joint funeral was held for Hugh and Humphrey some time later. According to a report in Y Glorian: 'Francis Hughes is now on his way back, having left the bodies of his loved ones far from home.'

A fund was set up locally to support the families with the aid of the Civic Council and the Churches. A letter of thanks from Francis Hughes was published in Y Glorian:

Sir – Would you be so kind as to allow me a few lines in your paper, so that I may express my thanks to the many neighbours and friends who have given support and sympathy to myself and my family in the grievous loss of my three sons. I have received a flood of letters and

Gravestone of the three brothers

personal expressions of sympathy, and I can never reply to them all nor express my appreciation. The loss of three sons in the flower of youth was a great blow to my wife and myself, but the great kindness and sympathy has helped us bear our grief. I thank you all, on behalf of my wife, my remaining children, and myself.

        Yours in sorrow.

        Francis Hughes

Francis Hughes was born in Nant Gwynant, but was raised at Morfa Bychan, and spent his career as a carpenter in the Oakley Quarry. Winifred, his wife, was also from Morfa Bychan and was also a sister to my grandfather Griffith Humphrey Jones, another who had already moved south to search for work and had settled at Ynyshir, Rhondda by 1913 before returning to Borth y Gest in the 1920s.

Aled L. Ellis (Minffordd, Penrhyndeudraeth), *Llafar Bro*, July 2012

Gwynedd's losses

All Penrhyn men safe

Penrhyndeudraeth, Friday

When news of the explosion reached Penrhyndeudraeth, an anxious time was spent fearing there might be local men among the dead. Mercifully, as far as we know, everyone from this town has been brought out, alive and safe.

Commercial Street, Senghennydd

Three Bethesda boys

Bethesda, Saturday

It is with great sorrow that we record the deaths of three young men of Bethesda. Two of them were George Davies and Ellis David, sons of Mr William Davies, Coetmor Terrace. George Davies was twenty-eight years old and had been working in the south for ten years, and Ellis his brother was twenty-one years old and had been working in the colliery for seven years. The other young man was William Williams, son of Thomas John Williams, Caeberllan, who was twenty-five years old and had worked for four years in the south. Before that he worked for some years in Penrhyn Quarry. William Williams had only moved from Abercynon to work in Senghenydd six months ago. Sympathy is extended to their families in their grievous loss.

An anxious wait in the Nantlle Valley

Penygroes, Saturday

The great disaster has cast its shadow over the Nantlle Valley. The weakness of the slate trade drove many locals to South Wales. Naturally, there was great anxiety in the valley when we heard the sad news. The streets of Penygroes were packed, and everyone rushed to the newsagent's for the latest news, but every copy was sold in no time. We understand that many men from Nantlle are working in Senghenydd and Abertridwr ...

Yr Herald Cymraeg, October 21 (1913), 8 col. 6

A woman identifying the body of her husband

The rescue of a father and son from Ffestiniog

Another father and son from Ffestiniog, John Owen Jones and his son Evan, were rescued, according to *Y Drych*:

From Ffestiniog
Evan told a reporter from *Banerau ac Amserau Cymru*:

I had only been working underground for fourteen months. When the explosion happened, we heard a terrible noise, followed by the sound of falling rocks. There was air sweeping through the pit, but it was full of dust and smoke. My own lamp and my son's lamp went out, and we gave up all hope. That being so, we decided to die together. Now and again we wet each other's lips with water from a bottle that we had, and no doubt that kept us alive till the rescue party came.

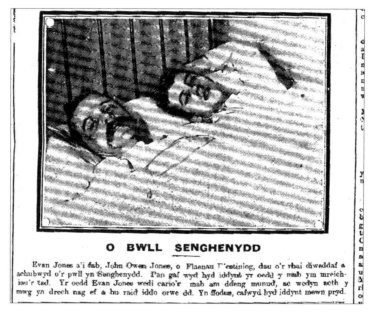

O BWLL SENGHENYDD

Evan Jones a'i fab, John Owen Jones, o Flaenau Ffestiniog, dau o'r rhai diweddaf a achubwyd o'r pwll yn Senghenydd. Pan gafwyd hyd iddynt yr oedd y mab ym mreichiau'r tad. Yr oedd Evan Jones wedi cario'r mab am ddeng munud, ac wedyn aeth y mwg yn drech nag ef a bu raid iddo orwedd. Yn ffodus, cafwyd hyd iddynt mewn pryd.

A photograph of John Owen Jones and his son Evan in Y Genedl

The Llan Band and the Great War
John Owen Jones and his son belonged to a talented family of bandsmen. His brother was the leader of Ystradgynlais band and a well-known cornet player. After being rescued from Senghenydd,

116

the father and son returned home to Llan Ffestiniog and rejoined the Llan Band.

According to John Hughes of Blaenau, a descendant of the family, the entire Llan Band joined the army when war broke out in 1914. For a year, the band was stationed in Park Hall camp, Oswestry, and took part in parades and recruitment drives. But because the army had suffered such heavy losses, the musicians soon had to become ordinary soldiers, and fight on various fronts.

Having escaped with his life from the Senghenydd explosion, Ifan Goronwy (Evan) was sent to the Dardanelles, and was killed there.

A Llanllyfni father and son
This distressing tale comes from 78-year-old Ellen Pritchard of Tal-y-sarn, Caernarfon. Her uncle, brother of her late mother, Lizzie Mary Jones, was killed in the explosion.

> I lost an uncle in the explosion. He was only nineteen years old, and my mother's brother. His name was Richard Owen Jones, and he and his father went from Arfon to South Wales to look for employment, because it was difficult to find work in the north at the time. His father's name was also Richard Jones.
>
> My mother often spoke of them having to go down south, though sadly I never knew either of them. They were lodgers in a house in

Richard Jones, the father, with his daughter Katie (another of Richard O. Jones's sisters). The father, mother and two of their friends would sometimes walk home to Llanllyfni from the coal mines. They would do so on moonlit nights, which allowed more time for walking.

117

Senghenydd, but my mother did not know the address.

When my grandmother, who lived with her six children in No 17, Rhedyw Road, Llanllyfni, Penygroes, Arfon, North Wales, heard of the accident, she was led to believe that her husband, Richard Jones, had died. It was, I think, on receipt of the second telegram that she realised a mistake had been made, and that the victim was in fact her son, Richard O. Jones. For some reason the two had swapped shifts.

When my sister and I were at a National Eisteddfod in the south many years ago, we and our father had the privilege of visiting

Er Serchog Goffadwriaeth

AM

— RICHARD O. JONES,

ANWYL FAB RICHARD AC ELLEN JONES, 17, RHEDYW ROAD, LLANLLYFNI,

Yr hwn a fu farw (yn y Welsh Pit Explosion, Universal Mine, Senghenydd,) Hydref 14, 1913,

Yn 19 Mlwydd Oed,

Ac a gladdwyd yn Penyrheol Cemetery, Hydref 18fed.

Richard O. Jones's memorial card

118

Penyrheol Cemetery where my uncle lay buried. The cemetery was by the side of the road, and looked quite tidy. There was a small office inside the cemetery and a gentleman who worked there as clerk/labourer. He looked up our uncle's name in a big book. We did not have to go far, because the slate gravestone could almost be seen from the office door. After we'd taken a photo or two, we went into the ancient little church nearby.

Many years later, when Dei, my husband, and I took the family on holiday, we would take flowers to the cemetery. But, as often happens these days, there were many acts of vandalism, and the little church had suffered. There was also a communal grave in the cemetery, but my uncle was laid in his own lonely grave, far from his home and family in 17 Rhedyw Road, Llanllyfni. According to Mam, my grandmother never saw her dear son's grave, which was a great shame.

In the Register of Deaths, the lodging house to which Ellen Pritchard refers is listed as 134 Caerphilly Road. Five generations of the family still remember Ellen Pritchard's grandfather and his son Richard O. Jones.

Caerphilly Road today

The sister at her brother's graveside – Lizzie Mary Jones beside Richard O. Jones's gravestone

Ellen Pritchard taking her children, David and Gillian, to visit Uncle Richard's grave for the first time

Ellen, her husband David and their children visit the grave

A family of lead miners, Bont-goch, Ceredigion

Arthur, Edwin and Tom were the sons of William Edwin Morris and his wife Elizabeth from Bont-goch, near Tal-y-bont. All three moved to 43 High Street, Abertridwr and found work in the Universal Colliery, Senghenydd. Edwin, aged twenty-three, and Tom, aged nineteen, were killed in the explosion on 14 October, 1913.

Bont-goch had a history of lead mining that spanned 300 years, from its beginnings in 1620. The heyday of the industry was the middle of the nineteenth century, when there were six mines in the area and the population was increasing. By the beginning of the twentieth century, only one mine was left, and that was Bwlch-glas, which closed in 1921.

The three young men came from a Ceredigion lead-mining family. The history of the family has been researched by Richard E. Huws and the Reverend Dr David H. Williams, Aberystwyth, and published in Papur Pawb, June 2001. Edwin and Elizabeth were married on 27 July 1888 in St Peter's Church, Elerch.

Bwlch-glas lead mine, Bont-goch

An old cage that carried the miners down Bwlch-glas shaft

Pen-yr-heol cemetery, near Abertridwr

The monument to the miners
who could not be identified

Gravestones of others lost in the disaster

At the time William worked as a labourer on Llety-Ifan-hen farm. His wife, Elizabeth, a local girl, was a widow and a maidservant in Pant-y-ffin. Her first husband was John Jones, Rhyd-yr-onnen, a lead miner, and the two were married at Elerch Church on 25 November, 1878. Elizabeth's parents were David Davies, a lead miner of Pant-y-celyn, and his wife, Elizabeth. The remains of Pant-y-ffin can still be seen on Bwlch Rosser bank, and the ruins of Rhyd-yr-onnen and Pant-y-celyn stand on the roadside between Cwmere and Moelgolomen.

By 1898, the father, William Edwin, was also a lead miner, but by 1901 he had left the mines of Ceredigion and become a collier in the Rhondda, lodging at 65 East Road, Ferndale. Three of the sons followed their father south. After suffering the horror of the Senghenydd accident, Arthur volunteered for the army at the beginning of the Great War:

In less than a year the bloody battles of the Great War began, and early on in the conflict Arthur Morris enlisted for military service. He probably thought that the war would be some sort of escape from the dangers of the coal mine, since he had just lost two brothers in the Universal pit disaster. In time, he left for France with the good wishes of the members of Senghenydd Wesleyan Church who presented him with a Bible and a hymn book to comfort him on his way. Afer two years in the trenches in France he was badly injured. He was allowed home to Bont-goch to convalesce, and was given a hero's welcome by the people of the locality. When he had recovered sufficiently, he spent some time with the army in Ireland in 1916, the year of the Easter Rebellion, before returning once more to France in June 1917. He died on the battlefield on 26 August 1918, leaving his parents to mourn the loss of their third son in less than five years.

The family lived in Elerch House till at least 1920, but I am not sure what became of them nor where they are buried. Arthur Morris is not commemorated on the Tal-y-bont war memorial, but his name appears on a memorial which is now part of Nazareth community centre, Abertridwr.

Gwilym Morgan Rees from Maesteg

Gwilym Rees left his home at 80 High Street, Senghenydd, on Tuesday morning, 14 October 1913, leaving his pregnant wife and two children, Cynwyd, who was two years old and Islwyn who was seven months old.

Gwilym Rees was twenty-nine years old. He was from Nantyffyllon, near Maesteg, and the son of Thomas and Mary Rees. Thomas Rees worked as a miner in the iron industry and then a coalminer. In 1867, when he was twenty-one years old, he married Mary Anthony, one of girls from Penlan farm, near Nantyffyllon. Later in his life, Thomas Rees set up a clothes shop the Beehive Stores in Nantyffyllon.

Thomas and Mary Rees had thirteen children. Eight of them died in infancy, as babies and children. Only two girls, Mary Ann and Jennet, and three sons, Gwilym, Taliesyn and Nehemiah, the last three to be born, reached adulthood.

Thomas Rees was active in the community. He was one of the pillars of Siloh Chapel, Nantyffyllon. In 1910, he was awarded the silver Sunday School medal for sixty years of service to the Sunday School at Siloh and he was a deacon of the chapel for over forty years. He represented the Nantyffyllon Ward on the Maesteg Town Council and was a member

Gwilym Rees in his Glamorgan Constabulary uniform, taken around March 1906

of the committee which was formed to establish a hospital for the Maesteg area.

It appears that Thomas Rees was not keen for his sons to work underground. At the time of the 1901 census, Gwilym, who was seventeen years old, was working as a railway porter and Taliesyn, who was 15 years old, worked as an assistant in a grocer's shop. After he left school, Nehemiah went to work with his Dad in the "Beehive" shop.

The Thomas family and Mary Rees – from left to right:
their son, Taliesyn Rees and, in front of him, his wife Mary Hannah;
their daughter, Jennet and her husband, David Evans behind her;
Thomas Rees and his wife Mary in front of him;
their daughter, Mary Ann and her husband Howell Thomas behind her; their son Gwilym Rees and his wife Elizabeth in front of him; and their son Nehemiah Rees.
The children of Mary Ann and Howell Thomas are the children seen in the picture – from left to right: Islwyn, Frances and Gwladys

On 6th January 1906, twenty-one years old and working as a grocer, Gwilym joined the Glamorgan Police. He is described, according to the police records, as six feet tall and with dark brown hair and grey eyes. He was appointed to work as a policeman in the Senghenydd area and lived there in the police station. It's more than likely that he met Elizabeth Jane Hodge, who lived at 32 Park Terrace, in Senghenydd, and they married in Bethel Chapel, Caerphilly on 27 September 1909. Her father was a coalminer, William Thomas Hodge.

In Loving Memory of

GWILYM M. REES,

Who lost his life in the Senghenydd Explosion, October 14th, 1913.

In health and strength he left his home,
Not thinking Death so near;
It pleased the Lord to bid him come,
And in His sight appear.

In prime of life he was cut down,
No longer could he stay;
Because it was his Saviour's will,
To call him hence away.

Aged 29 Years.

A copy of the funeral leaflet

However, Gwilym Rees' life changed within six weeks of the wedding because, on 12 November, 1909, after serving in the police for almost four years, he resigned and went to work in the Universal coalmine in Senghenydd. At the time of the 1911 Census, he was working as a Coal Weigher and, at the time of the explosion, as an Assistant Repairer (according to the report in the press of his funeral) and as a Timber man's helper (according to the death certificate). Despite this, having worked there for three years, he had decided to re-join the police and he was waiting to restart with the police when he died in the explosion. His coffin was carried by members of the Glamorgan Police Force when his funeral was held in Senghenydd and in Llangynwyd church graveyard, Maesteg, where he was buried on Sunday, 20th November 1913. According to his death certificate, he died of 'Burns and suffocation following explosion of fire damp at Universal Colliery Senghenydd due to accident'.

His third son – named Gwilym, after his father – was born on 28 March 1914. The family of Thomas Rees was a great support to Gwilym's widow and her children, but the life of Thomas Rees was further shattered on November 6th 1915 with the death at the age of twenty-seven, after a long illness, of his youngest son, Nehemiah, who should have inherited the Beehive business. Thomas Rees gave up the business more or less immediately after this, and went with his wife to live with their daughter, Jennet and her son-in-law, David Evans, at 1 Garnwen Road, Nantyffyllon, on Christmas Eve 1915. He died in July 1921 at the age of seventy-five, and left in his will £20 each for Gwilym's children when they reached twenty-one years old,

John 'Clogs' in the Talardd pub, Llanllwni

which is the equivalent of some £700 these days. Mary Rees died on December 21st 1923 at the age of seventy-six.

What happened to Gwilym's children?

Cynwyd, the oldest son, got married in 1938 to Irene Griffiths, from Senghenydd, and they had a daughter, Glenda, in Birmingham, in the summer of 1939. Cynwyd joined the army, at the time of the Second World War, serving with the Royal Army Service Corps, but he died at Dunkirk on 29 May 1940. So, like his father before him, he didn't live to see his children grow to be adults.

With the depression of the 30s in the last century, the two other sons also went to live in Birmingham. The youngest son, Gwilym, died there in 1945, at the age of thirty and unmarried. Islwyn, the second son, married and he and his wife had two daughters, Maureen and Jeanette. Islwyn died in Birmingham in 1976 at the age of sixty-three, but throughout his life he kept in touch with the family of his aunt Jennet and her husband, David Evans, who had supported him and his brother when they were children

Wyn Rees

'Tad-cu' from the Rhondda, 'Taid' from Talsarnau

It is strange how just naming a place at times can silence everyone around. John 'Clogs' Jones was in the Talardd pub, in Llanllwni, Carmarthenshire – a pub he runs with Anne his wife – entertaining the customers with his interesting stories, and one of the crew asked, 'Where do you come from originally, John.'

And the answer was 'Senghenydd'.

This opened the floodgates to many childhood memories and stories about his 'tad-cu' (grandfather, south Wales) and 'taid' (grandfather, north Wales) who worked in the coalmine at the time of the tragedy:

Eic Williams – from the Rhondda originally – was working a

night shift at the Universal before the explosion. There were no benefits at that time and the custom was that a coalminer would work double shifts for his partner if he couldn't go to work because of sickness or some other reason. He would give the pay for that shift to the family of his partner. Well, when Eic went to the top that morning he was searching for his partner all over the place. His partner's wife was expecting a baby about that time and if he hadn't been able to go to work that morning, Eic would have worked a double shift in his place. When Eic was about to turn back to go underground, he saw his partner running towards him

Eic Williams (who died in 1958) with Mam-gu (Grandmother)

happily and saying that everything is alright, that the baby had arrived safely during the night and there would be no need for Eic to work a double shift after all. And the new father went below ground.

Eic walked home over the mountain to his terraced house in Treharris. The first he knew of the accident was when a neighbour came to knock on the door to ask his wife if Eic was safe in bed – the news about the tragedy had arrived.

Taid – John Vaughan Jones, originally from Llandecwyn, Merionethshire – was underground in the Bottanic on that morning. He was a young man, working with the ponies in the company of an experienced jostler.

The wind direction changed on the level and the ponies were unsettled, and they must have heard something too. "Something's happened," said the old boy, "we'd better not move until someone comes to look for us." And there were the two of them when the rescue team arrived in the end. Only after getting to the surface of the works and seeing the hundreds and hundreds who were there waiting for some news did they realise the extent of the explosion. In the middle of the crowd were Nain and my father – Tecwyn – a baby of three months old in her arms, and a little sister. And only two walked out of the cage.

A year after that, Taid went to the army – he was recruited in the merriment of the propaganda in Caerphilly and he sent a message home with someone else to say that he had gone to the war. He was in the Welsh Cavalry with his horse Pickles, throughout the war and he arrived home without a mark on his skin and a great hero. But these important experiences had scarred him too. He would spend six months working, going to chapel and everything like that – and then six months drinking. His wife was buried young and the children were scattered between relatives in Liverpool and Hereford.

Tecwyn – my father – worked on the telephone wires underground in the Abertridwr pit. It was always warm underground – but sometimes he would have to go up to the old level in the Universal in Senghenydd. It was an old 'escape route' and he would say that it was a horrible experience. It was so quiet and so cold there.

We were living in High Street, Senghenydd. I remember Mam-gu – Eic's wife – answering someone who asked her, 'It must be a very sad place.' This was true of course, between the explosion, the war, the great strike and the depression – but the answer Mam-gu gave, 'Yes, but laughter and singing come back.'

The boy next door had been in the gas on the underground level but he survived because he wetted his cap and held it over his mouth and breathed through it until the rescue team got to him. Years later he was interviewed for the television on some programme, and whilst telling this story he pulled his cap off his head and held it over his mouth. Well, no-one in the village had seen the man without his cap before and that was the talking point for some time: 'Did you see him with his cap? His big bald head shining on telly!'

When I was fourteen years old, we moved to Dwyran, Anglesey. I had an aunt living there – her husband was a sailor from Newborough and he had worked in the Abertridwr pit for some time before they moved back to Anglesey. It was 1960 when they moved – there was no further education for a lad of fifteen in Senghenydd at that time. He had no choice but to leave and go to the works. But Dad brought us to Anglesey so that I could have a few more years of education.

John Vaughan Jones (standing) with his friend after joining the army in Caerphilly in 1914/5

CG 009886

CERTIFIED COPY of   an ENTRY OF BIRTH
COPI DILYS O   GOFNOD GENEDIGAETH

Pursuant to the Births and   **Deaths Registration Act 1953**

Registration District | Ffestiniog
Dosbarth Cofrestru |

1885	BIRTH in the Sub-district of GENEDIGAETH yn Is-ddosbarth	Llanfihangelyffraethau				in the County of Merioneth yn		
Columns: Colofnau:	1	2	3	4	5	6	7	8	9
No. Rhif	When and where born Pryd a Be y ganwyd	Name, if any Enw os oes un	Sex Rhyw	Name, and surname of father Enw a chyfenw'r tad	Name, surname, and maiden surname of mother Enw, cyfenw a chyfenw morwynol y fam	Occupation of father Gwaith y tad	Signature, description, and residence of informant Llofnod, disgrifiad a chyfeiriad yr hysbysydd	When registered Pryd y cofrestrwyd	Signature Llofnod cofrestrydd
51	Tenth April 1885 Tolsarnau Llanfihangel R.S.D.	John Vaughan	Boy	Richard Vaughan Jones	Mary Jones formerly Richards	Farmer	Richard V. Jones Father Talsarnau Llanfihangel	Twenty-nine April 1885	Rees Robe... Registrar

John Vaughan Jones's birth certificate in Talsarnau, Merionethshire

A little collier boy

In their home in High Street, Abertridwr, Bill and Barbara Tudor have amassed a wealth of information on the miners in the family, as well as photographs of Senghenydd and the explosion. They have created a family archive, that includes copies of birth certificates and the relevant entries in the 1911 census, so that the story can be passed on to the next generation, one of whom is their granddaughter Carys from Pontypridd, a student of Welsh at Bangor University.

Bill Tudor, Abertridwr

Bill Tudor was born in 1928, the year that the Universal pit finally closed. His father, Thomas, worked in the pit, but survived the explosion. His father's brother, 14-year-old Alfred Rees Tudor, was killed. Bill has been able to show Carys her great-great-uncle's name on the 1911 Census, when he was aged twelve. As was usual at that time the family had two lodgers, who had moved to the area to find work. According to the Census one was born in Ceredigion and the other in Aberdare.

Bill has acquired copies of old newspaper reports from local libraries and from Cardiff. He also has a copy of Alfred's death certificate. The young man is described as 'Collier boy of No 33 Alexandra Terrace, Senghenydd' and the cause of death is: 'Burns and suffocation following explosion of fire damp at Universal Colliery Senghenydd due to accident'.

Barbara was born in the house next door to her present home. Three brothers who were killed in the explosion – Joseph (twenty-seven), David (twenty-four) and Llewelyn Williams (twenty-one) – lived at that same address. David Williams was married to Katie who was one of Barbara's schoolteachers. Katie took up teaching again after the death of her husband.

Another strand in the family story is that of the Welsh language.

Barbara's grandfather, Robert Edwards of Blaenau Ffestiniog, came to the Rhymney valley to work in the coal mines, before moving on to Senghenydd. Barbara's mother could speak Welsh, and so too could Bill's mother. Although their own generation missed out on the language, they made sure that their children were educated in Welsh and are delighted that Carys and her generation speak it fluently.

CERTIFIED COPY of COPI DILYS O Pursuant to the Births and						an ENTRY OF DEATH GOFNOD MARWOLAETH Deaths Registration Act 1953		WHD 012308	

Registration District / Dosbarth Cofrestru: Pontyprida

1914. Death in the Sub-district of / Marwolaeth yn Is-ddosbarth: Eglwysilan in the County of Glamorgan

No. Rhif	When and where died Pryd a lle y bu farw	Name and surname Enw a chyfenw	Sex Rhyw	Age Oed	Occupation Gwaith	Cause of death Achos marwolaeth	Signature, description and residence of informant Llofnod, disgrifiad a chyfeiriad yr hysbysydd	When registered Pryd y cofrestrwyd	Signature of registrar Llofnod y cofrestrydd
†96	14th October 1913 Universal Colliery Senghenydd Caerphilly UD	Alfred Rees Tudor	Male	14 years	Collier Boy of No 33 Alexandra Terrace Senghenydd	Burns and Suffocation following explosion of fire damp at Universal Colliery Senghenydd due to accident	Certificate received from David Rees Coroner for East Glamorgan Inquest held 27th January 1914	Second February 1914	C.M Nicholas Deputy Registrar

Certified to be a true copy of an entry in a register in my custody.
Tystiolaethwyd ei fod yn gopi cywir o gofnod mewn cofrestr a gedwir gennyf i.   E Lewis   Deputy Superintendent Registrar / Cofrestrydd Arolygol   10·10·2007   Date / Dyddiad

CAUTION: THERE ARE OFFENCES RELATING TO FALSIFYING OR ALTERING A CERTIFICATE AND USING OR POSSESSING A FALSE CERTIFICATE. ©CROWN COPYRIGHT
GOFAL: MAE YNA DROSEDDAU YN YMWNEUD Â FFUGIO NEU ADDASU TYSTYSGRIF NEU DDEFNYDDIO TYSTYSGRIF FFUG NEU WRTH FOD AG UN YN EICH MEDDIANT. ©HAWLFRAINT Y GORON
WARNING: A CERTIFICATE IS NOT EVIDENCE OF IDENTITY.
RHYBUDD: NID YW TYSTYSGRIF YN PROFI PWY YDYCH CHI.

E 26

Alfred Rhys Tudor's death certificat

CENSUS OF ENGLAND AND WALES, 1911.

The 1911 Census

Thomas Edward Tudor (Bill's father) was born in Aberdare and spoke Welsh,
but the other children only spoke English. Two miners lodged with the family,
one from Ceredigion and one from Aberdare. Both were Welsh speakers.
Alfred Rhys Tudor, the boy who was killed, was twelve years old at the time of the Census

In health and strength they left their homes,
Not thinking death so near;
It pleased the Lord to bid them come,
And in His sight appeared.

JOSEPH WILLIAMS

DAVID WILLIAMS

LLEWELYN WILLIAMS

In Loving Memory of

JOSEPH WILLIAMS, Aged 27 Years;

DAVID WILLIAMS, Aged 24 Years;

LLEWELYN WILLIAMS, Aged 21 Years

The Beloved Sons of MARY WILLIAMS.

Who Died on the 14th day of October, 1913.

And were interred at Penyrheol Cemetery, 17th November 1913.

66 High Street,
Abertridwr.

The memorial card of the three Abertridwr brothers

Bill and Barbara sharing the story with their granddaughter,
Carys

From the quarries of the Eifl
John Celyn Jones

At the beginning of the twentieth century John Celyn Jones was a quarryman in Llithfaen. He was a poet, who composed personal greetings for the local press, and hymns and religious songs for Trysorfa'r Plant and denominational magazines. He won a chair in the in the Youth Eisteddfod of his local area in 1911, and also wrote political verses on the battles of the quarrymen for their rights.

He came to prominence as the secretary of his union, and later turned to insurance and

John Celyn Jones

charity work to assist men who suffered as a result of industrial accidents. An accident involving a family member may well have brought home to him the importance of such work. Here is a report from *Yr Herald Cymraeg*:

The Llithfaen Accident
While he was going about his work in the Eifl quarry last Monday, Robert Jones, Bryn Celyn, met with a terrible accident, when a rock fell on his head causing a deep wound. There is no doubt that he would have died there and then, were it not for the ability of Mr Aidan Davies, who is known as a skilled member of 'St John Ambulance'.

Celyn contributed a weekly column of local news to *Y Genedl Gymreig*, but in October 1913 he moved to Caerphilly to undertake insurance and charity work amongst the workers of the neighbouring valleys. Ironically he arrived in the area in the very week of the Senghenydd explosion. His last two contributions to *Y Genedl* were a description of preparations for his journey to south Wales, followed by a report on the deaths and funerals in Senghenydd:

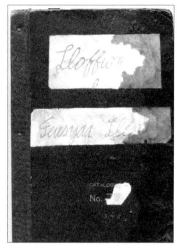

A collection of clippings of John Celyn Jones' work

Next day, I went to Abertridwr and Senghenydd, the sorrowful place where the explosion took place, and what a sorrowful place it was. The curtains were drawn in almost every other house, and families were waiting at the pit head for the bodies of their loved ones to be brought up for burial. There was a stack of fine coffins ready to receive the victims, some of whom were waiting to be identified. I saw the biggest funeral I have ever seen. Think of spending a whole hour watching one single funeral procession! Members of the Friendly Society to which the young man belonged, many men on horseback, a brass band, and an almost innumerable crowd followed the coffin. I doffed my hat, without knowing why, and as I looked upon his coffin covered in flowers, his folded military uniform, and his wife and small children following behind, I couldn't hold back the tears.

From the Place of Funerals
(a letter from Senghenydd)

It is with the greatest seriousness and solemnity that I use the above title, and I believe that the events of these last weeks in the Caerphilly area, especially Senghenydd, fully justify that name. Since this black period in the history of the region is fast drawing to a close, as far as burying the victims is concerned, and since the country and its newspapers have to some extent moved on to other matters of more or less importance, I believe that a short account of the aftermath of the explosion would be of interest.

The past weeks have been a time of worry, sadness and grief for scores of families, who have had to give up all hope of seeing their loved ones alive. Daily they have had to prepare themselves for the return of the bodies. Daily they have gone to the pit head and searched anxiously through the few trinkets that belonged to the victims, as this is now the only means of identifying the bodies. Many sons and fathers and lodgers have been identified by a box or key or pocket knife. Then there is the appearance of the 'black car' bearing the coffin home, with crowds lining the road, most out of curiosity, others who can sympathise from the bottom of their hearts.

Mourning dress

This is the most flourishing trade at the present time; the shops have only 'black clothes' on display. They are bought by mothers and children (no fathers), ready for the time when the head of the family's body is found, for the bodies are buried as soon as they are brought to the surface, and the graves have already been dug. In every cemetery there are rows of open graves (is this not the 'harvest of death'?) In one cemetery I counted over 200 open graves, and many already filled. A decoration, made by a gentle hand and hanging on the end wall of the church, caught the mood. It showed a picture of an old coalmine, embroidered with flowers on a black cloth.

The Funerals

It wasn't just one or two or three of the above that made their way to Eglwysilan Church, Penyrheol, and Caerphilly every day, especially on Sunday, and who would deny them that day for the burial of the dead? Those were the most powerful sermons I ever heard, and it was strange how they touched every heart. You'd see the crowd joining a procession without even asking whose funeral it was. The 'black miner' deserves respect and admiration for his readiness to pay his last respects to a fellow-worker in this way. Although the funerals differ slightly from each other, they are all popular. Here is a list of the different funerals I witnessed.

The Unknown Miner

This undoubtedly is the saddest. With no one there to shed tears of true grief! Because no one knows who he is! The victim is taken straight from the pit to the cemetery. The crowd follows the coffin knowing only that it contains one of 'the colliery martyrs', who may be a loved one or a friend. The victim is buried with all due ceremony and respect. There is nothing to mark his grave. Nothing but the number on his coffin. The bodies are numbered when found by the brave rescuers who have been searching for them. It is heartbreaking to hear how they came upon the contorted bodies of their friends. These good men deserve better pay than that offered by the company for their work. Recognition by the Crown is no less than they deserve.

The Lodger's Funeral

This is another sombre funeral. A young man, far from home, borne from his lodging house in a coffin, with one or two family members present to pay their last respects; others with parents who are too poor or too old to attend. Let this be known far and wide: the householders of the south, to their great credit, do not make distinctions. The very same respect is paid to the funeral of the poor lodger, and he is laid to rest among his unfortunate brothers.

The Funeral of Fathers and Sons

This is no different from any funeral throughout the country. Sorrow and also great sadness due to the pressing need and concern for daily bread. It was so heartbreaking to see the mothers, who were mostly young, and their little children following the coffin in the hearse. Deep are the sighs and many the tears shed on the way to the various cemeteries.

The Soldier's Funeral

This the most dignified of all. The country is always keen to respect a soldier (at least when he's dead). The coffins are carried with great pomp on gun carriages. The military uniform lies folded on the coffin and is covered in wreaths. One, two, sometimes three brass bands lead the procession. Soldiers from all the surrounding areas are summoned to march in front of the coffin, all smartly dressed and looking most dignified. A crowd of thousands follows behind. This is a funeral that stays long in the memory. The gun salute at the graveside is sombre indeed, and strikes hard at the hearts of the victims' loved ones.

The Funeral of a Soldier of the Cross

This is the last one I witnessed, and the one that made the greatest impression on my busy mind. A young miner, who had been brave enough to bear witness to Christ in the colliery, and on the streets of Caerphilly, despite mockery and insults, and the swearing of the crowds. Everyone was in floods of tears. He left neither father, mother, brother nor sister to claim him on the Sabbath of his funeral. The Salvation Army burial service is very pleasing. Everyone dressed in blue with the banner of the Cross carried at the head of the procession and a brass band playing a solemn hymn. The Captain gave a glowing tribute to the young man at the graveside. He prayed to great effect. Then the crowd sang a hymn and everyone was in floods of tears. There was an element of comfort in this funeral and 'the balm of hope that eases pain'.

'Celyn', Caerphilly

The smallholders of Mynydd Bach, Ceredigion

Idris Morgan, a sheep farmer of Mynydd Bach, Ceredigion, has been looking into his family history. It's surprising to learn that the Senghenydd disaster also touched the lives of this rural family:

Charles Morgan, my paternal grandfather, lived near Troed-rhiw in Trefenter. After working as a cowman and labouring locally, my grandfather went to work on farms in neighbouring areas. He then realised that there were more opportunities and better pay in the mines of south Wales. Lewis, his brother, came up on a visit one day. Some of Lewis's friends in the coal mine found it difficult to break horses, not only the pit ponies but also the ones they kept on their smallholdings. Many of the colliers had smallholdings. There was no one like Charles for laying down a horse. He would grip the edge of his ear and his nose, and then his two arms would force the horse to buckle and fall. But Lewis was stronger still. When he was home working on the land, he could lift the plough or the mouldboard on his back and carry them over fences from one field to the next without a second thought.

Charles was coming to the end of his term of employment which made it easier for Lewis to persuade him to move away. Off they went to the colliery with their boxes of clothes. They were also taken by pony and trap around various farms. On some farms there'd be five or six two year-old horses waiting to be broken. For a while the two of them worked with the horses as well as working in the mine.

Colliery horses were often unmanageable and needed to be tamed. At that time horse owners would send any wild horse, or a horse that had 'bolted' or was obstinate, to the mart in Llanybydder, or maybe in Ffair Rhos. Any horse that was bought would be sent on to the mine.

The pit where Charles worked was known for being oppressively hot underground. It was so hot that the colliers only wore underpants. Then one day they might be summoned to work on the surface where it was freezing cold. The sudden change of temperature cost many their lives. My grandfather came home and very nearly died. Though suffering from pneumonia he caught the train from Treorchy and walked the eight or nine miles home from Tregaron station.

Idris Morgan

It was leeches that saved his life. In fact, Charles became an expert at breeding leeches and hiring them out to the sick who wanted to get rid of bad blood. He would buy the leeches from the chemist, or druggist, as he called him. He became interested in leeches after he'd used them to save his own life. Leeches are once again being used to cure the sick. Charles kept leeches for years, and was known for it far and wide.

Charles's eldest brother, Dafydd, went with his family to Senghenydd. Dafydd and his fifteen year-old son were killed in the disaster of 1913. After he lost his brother and nephew, Charles took his horse and little cart all the way to Senghenydd to pick up the family and their few belongings and bring them back to Trefenter. As the head of the family had been killed, the widow and children were turned out of their home. The colliery owner was also the owner of the miners' cottages.

The widow and youngest children found refuge in Tan-y-foel on Parish land. And if my grandfather hadn't been able to butcher meat, they'd have died of starvation. They fed themselves on stew made from sheep's heads and bones. Neighbours would supply potatoes and vegetables to keep them going.

Idris Morgan, Mynydd Bach

Fund-raising

Across the nation fund-raising began, in various ways. People were used to this – according to the *County Echo* (Pembrokeshire), in the previous fifty years £862,548 had been raised in connection with thirty-three colliery disasters. Because the number of claimants had decreased over the years, there was a balance of £100,000, and proposals were being made for the use of that money for Senghenydd.

In Dinas Cross, where Tom Mendus had lived, there was a 'collection on foot'.

The Goodwick Brass Bank held two parades in Fishguard, one in pouring rain, assisted by the Boy Scouts. They collected £4 11s on the first parade and £3 on the second; two more were planned.

Lampeter raised £10 7s 6d; St Peter's Church, Carmarthen, £16 10s 9d.

The Welsh Football Association asked clubs to play for money for the relief fund. On 7 November a football match was arranged between Llandysul Town XI and Lampeter College XI to raise funds, and also in November Llandudno played Caernarfon.

The *Flintshire Observer/Mining Journal and General Advertiser* reported that in late October, Mold District Council had held a special meeting to discuss opening a relief fund; there is, surprisingly, little mention, other than this, in this newspaper.

In late October the Coronation Silver Band paraded round Barmouth and raised £4 4s; chapel collections were also being taken.

The Silver Band was also out in Newtown. They were used to fund-raising: they had raised money after the Titanic had sunk in 1912. They held a concert and raised £11 10s; when the Town Council was asked to contribute they simply requested yet another concert from the Silver Band.

A relief concert was held at the Aberystwyth Coliseum; performances at 3 p.m., 6.30 p.m. and 8.30 p.m. A total of £10 0s

Encl

13th Decr 1913.

My dear Sir,

Senghenydd Relief Fund.

I am in receipt of your letter of the 12th instant enclosing cheque value £506-4-2, representing the amount raised in Barry towards the above Fund, for which I am extremely obliged.

I have pleasure in forwarding herewith official receipt, and in doing so should like to express through you, to the inhabitants of Barry, my warm and sincere thanks for their kind and generous response to the appeal made on behalf of the sufferers of this sad and deplorable Colliery disaster.

May I also convey to you personally my sincere thanks for the assistance you have rendered to the Fund by your local appeal.

Believe me to be,

Yours very faithfully,

Robinson

Lord Mayor.

Councillor Thomas Davies,

Contribution of £506-4s-2d from Barry

6d was raised. Collections in the town amassed £25 0s 6d, and the Sunday School raised £10 4s.

Dr Barnardo's homes 'offered immediate admission to any number of children who have become orphans and been rendered destitute by this terrible catastrophe.' The local Superintendent had been to the village to talk to people; the Chief of Staff had been to Cardiff to make sure everything was in place to help anyone who needed help. 'The children will be admitted at the local branch of the Homes – the 'Ever-Open Door' at Cardiff – which is well known to all the local authorities.'

SENGHENYDD COLLIERY DISASTER
(BARRY RELIEF FUND)

THEATRE ROYAL, BARRY
(Kindly lent by Mr. Carlton for the occasion).

GRAND MISCELLANEOUS
CONCERTS
In aid of the above Fund, will be given on

THURSDAY, NOVEMBER 13, 1913
MATINÉE
KINDLY ARRANGED BY THE LADIES OF THE BARRY 20th CENTURY CLUB, FROM 3 TO 5.

Grand Evening Concert
AT 7.30

Chairman - T. DAVIES, Esq., J.P.

ARTISTES: (Chairman of the Barry Urban District Council)

Miss Nancy Wyles   Miss Alice Lewis
Miss Tegwen Davies   Mr. Edward H. Davies
Mr. Dan Evans, Mr. R. T. Williams, Mr. D. W. Jenkins
Barry Operatic Society   Romilly Boys' Choir
Apollo Octette   Gladstone Road Juvenile Choir
ETC., ETC.

Solo Violinist : Professor TOM JONES.   Accompanist : Mr. F. G. BENNETT

PRICES.

Stalls 2s.; Circle 1s.; Pit or Gallery 6d.

Rees Jones, Printer, Barry.

147

The inquest ... and the £24 fine

Senghennydd

I roamed the dull streets in the valley blind
With mist and rain and the murk colliery smoke,
Churches I saw that to the passer spoke
Of many a soul that for God's peace had pined.
And refuge from man's multitudinous pain:
But darker far upon the valley lay
Than colliery smoke the shadow of the day
That saw that holocaust of strong men slain
On Wealth's soiled altars. In a room hard by
The men of law were met, with Mammon's crew,
Lords of the money bags, in long debate
Of who's to blame, and how it fell and why
Those hundreds went to flaming death – and yet
Not one sat there but the whole secret knew!

Sonnet by T. Gwynn Jones
Translation by H. I. Bell

The inquest on the explosion was held on Monday 5 January 1914 by the coroner, David Rees, and lasted seven days. The jury released the verdict: Accidental Death.

Five men had died from the effects of burns, and of injuries. One rescuer died the following day in a rock fall. The other 434 were asphyxiated by carbon monoxide gas; many also had burns and multiple injuries.

With great reluctance, the government was forced to hold an enquiry into the explosion, and a commission was set up with R. A. S. Redmayne, H.M. Chief Inspector of Mines, as commissioner; Evan Williams represented the owners, and Robert Smillie the Miners'

Federation of Great Britain.

The inquiry interviewed fifty-two witnesses, with 21,837 questions being asked. Edward Shaw, the manager of Universal Colliery, came under particular scrutiny, and was interviewed over three days. If Mr Redmayne found discrepancies amongst the witnesses he would not hesitate in recalling them. In all the enquiry took nearly a month.

The conclusion was drawn that the explosion originated at the Mafeking Incline due to a heavy fall, which released methane gas. This was possibly ignited by electrical signalling apparatus, or a rock falling – or a defective safety lamp or matches, of which no evidence could be found.

This enquiry revealed an appalling disregard by the owners for safety and the Coal Mines Act. They had committed numerous breaches of this Act, including allowing coal dust to accumulate in the roadways, and not having provisions to reverse the surface fan.

Mr Redmayne stated:

I incline to the belief that if rescue apparatus had been kept at the colliery, and men equpped with breathing apparatus had at once penetrated the West York District by the return and the Bottanic District, a few more lives might have been saved. I am convinced that had there been available at the time an adequate water supply, and had the brigades of rescuers attacked the three fires, the fires might have been extinguished in a comparatively short time. I should have thought, in view of the fact that the colliery was such a gassy one, and as it had already been devastated by an explosion, that the management would have made arrangements for a supply of water adequate to meet an emergency of that kind.

Yet Redmayne did not fully condemn Edward Shaw, the manager:

Several of these breaches may appear trivial, but taken in the aggregate they point to a disquieting laxity in the management of the mine. I regret exceedingly having to say this because Mr Shaw impressed me as an honest, industrious and in many respects an active manager, and he gave me his evidence in a clear and straightforward manner and assisted the Inquiry to the utmost of his power.

It would be invidious, where all the mining engineers and miners engaged in attempted rescue operations worked so hard in endeavouring to get past the fire in the workings with the object of saving life, to commend individuals by name, but I think a particular need of praise is due to Mr Shaw and to the small band of workers who accompanied him underground immediately after the explosion.

Robert Smillie of the Miners' Federation was more direct, stating:

Immediate reversing of the air current ought to have taken place, which would have meant the saving of the lives of all the men in the West York District. Most of the men had found their way to within a short distance of the York pit when they were overcome by fumes.

Evan Williams, for the owners, naturally took a different view to that of the other two:

I am of the opinion that the explosion was not consequent upon any breach of the Act or Regulations, nor due to any lack of precaution of a kind not required by law. Other than that which may be attached to the position of the re-lighting station, and while there were some contraventions of the statute, they were all, with the exception of the failure to complete means for immediate reversing of the ventilation, of the nature of neglect to comply with formalities of no importance in themselves.

Again with great reluctance, the government agreed to prosecution; the manager was charged with seventeen breaches of the Coal Mines Act, and the Company charged with four breaches. All charges against the owners were dismissed, and of the charges against the manager only five carried convictions.

In May 1914 Edward Shaw was fined £10, £10, £2, and £2. A grand total of £24.

The local newspaper scathingly stated: 'Miners' Lives at 1s 1¼d each'. [The equivalent of 5½p in 2012.]

The Lewis Merthyr Consolidated Collieries were convicted on one count: that is, for not being able to reverse the main ventilation fan, which, according to Mr Smillie, cost over 100 lives. They were fined £10 with £5 5s costs.

Among the victims were eight lads who were fourteen years old; another sixty of the victims were under twenty years old.

Left behind were 205 widows, 542 children, and sixty-two dependent parents.

Universal Colliery was soon back in production, but not at the employment levels of pre-explosion times. In 1915 it employed 1,330 men, and in the period 1916–18 1,286 men, with Edward Shaw still the manager. The pit employed 1,731 men in 1923 and 1,286 men in 1927.

In November 1928 the company denied that they were dismantling the pit prior to closure. They claimed it was only partial dismantling, and that the opening up of other seams would be considered when trading conditions were more favourable.

It then closed for good.

The gravestones of Eglwys Ilan

(the parish church)
Note: most of the inscriptions on the stones are in capital letters. Some are in English, and some in Welsh.

1. *(marble scroll, very unclear)*

    In loving remembrance of / David Thomas / beloved husband of / E A Richards / Gelli Terrace, Senghenydd / who lost his life at the Senghenydd / explosion October 14th 1913 / Aged 38 years

    Also of their daughters / Margaretta / Died Nov 1904 Aged 3 years / Gretta died Dec 1907 Aged 1 month / Cassie died June 1911 Aged 5 months / Annetta died August 18th 1935 / Aged 28 years

    Also Elizabeth Ann / Died July 1954 Aged 80

2. *(father and son)*

    In loving memory / of / my beloved husband / William J Hyatt / who met his death in the Senghenydd explosion / Oct 14th 1913 aged 48 years

    Farewell dear wife so good and kind
    Pray love the children I left behind
    It was God's decree surely true
    That made me part so soon from you.

    Also Brinley Hyatt / beloved son of the above / who met his death in the Senghenydd explosion / Oct 14th 1913 Aged 22 years.
    Also George Hyatt / beloved son of the above / who died Oct 14, 1903, aged 8 years

Mynwent Eglwys Ilan

3. *(compare with the verses in 15 and 22)*

In loving memory / of / David John Lewis / the beloved husband of Mabel Lewis / 11 Bridgefield Street, Abertridwr / who lost his life at the / Senghenydd explosion / October 14th 1913 / aged 25 years.

A sudden chance – I in a moment fell,
I had no time to bid my friends farewell,
Make nothing strange: death happens unto all,
My lot today – tomorrow you may fall.

4. *(flat on the ground, some of the wording overgrown)*

In ... memory of / David / the beloved husband of / Margaret Hughes / 84 Thomas St Abertridwr / who lost his life at the / Senghenydd explosion / ... 14th 1913, aged 49 years

153

...ore be ye also ready: for in such
...as ye think not the son of m ...
...Matthew xxiv.44

Also of Clifford / son of the above / ...14th 1907 aged 10 weeks
....

5. *(clear and beautiful stone)*

Er serchus gof / am / Evan Evans / anwyl briod Sarah A. Evans / 6 Grove Terrace, Senghenydd / Bu farw yn Nhanchwa Senghenydd / Hydref 14 1913 / yn 44 mlwydd oed.

Hefyd am eu hanwyl blant / Evan, Annie Mary, a Meredith

"Gadewch i blant bychain ddyfod attaf fi."

6. *(two brothers)*

In loving memory of / John Davies / Aged 28 years / and / George Davies / aged 19 years / Sons of William & Mary Ann Davies / Station Terrace, Senghenydd / who lost their lives in the / Universal Colliery explosion / Oct 14th 1913

"Therefore be ye also ready, for in such an hour as / ye think not the son of ma cometh."

Also Mary Ann Owens / beloved mother of the above / who died Oct 8th 1936 / aged 80 years

Rest in Peace

7. In loving memory of / Ivor George Lewis / who entered into rest / November 26 – 1911, aged 4 months.

Also John Lewis / beloved husband of Mary Jane Lewis / who

met his death in the Senghenydd explosion / Oct 14 – 1913, aged 35 years

Farewell dear wife this life is past
You dearly loved me to the last,
Grieve not for me nor sorrow take
But love my children for my sake

Mary Jane Baker / Died 17th Dec 1970, aged 93 years

Benjamin Lewis / Died 21st June 1976 aged 62 years

8. In loving memory of / Henry / the beloved husband of / Gwenllian Boswell / Senghenydd / who met his death at the / Universal Colliery Oct 14th 1913 / aged 54 years

Also of Amy, their daughter / who died Dec 27th 1911 aged 22 years

"Thy will be done"

9. *(clear and beautiful stone)*

Er serchus gof / am / Griffith Roberts / mab Morris a Ellen Roberts / 40 Stanley Street, Senghenydd / bu farw yn Nhanchwa / Senghenydd / Hydref 14. 1913 / yn 21 mlwydd oed.

10. In loving memory of / Henry Davies / High St, Abertridwr / who met his death at the / Senghenydd Colliery / Oct 14th 1913 aged 33 years.

"Thy will be done"

11. *(father and son; beautiful stone)*

In loving memory of / William / the beloved husband of / Elizabeth Ann Ross / Senghenydd / who lost his life in the / Senghenydd Colliery explosion / Oct 14th 1913, aged 46 years

Also their dearly beloved son / William John / who lost his life Oct 14th 1913 / aged 23 years

God touched them and they slept.

Also / Elizabeth Ann Taylor / (nee Ross) / who passed away Dec 13 – 1954 / aged 82 years

Also / Richard John Davies / infant

12. *(the same family as 11.; another lovely stone)*

In loving memory of / Peter Donald / the beloved husband of / Charlotte Ross / Senghenydd / who lost his life in the / Senghenydd Colliery explosion / Oct 14th 1913, aged 21 years

Alas: How Brief

13. *(?, the date is right, but there is no reference to the explosion)*

In loving memory of / Elizabeth Short / Died May 22, 1951 / Devoted mother of her children.

Also / James Smith / Brother of the above died Oct 14, 1913

But the Lord hath nought amiss
And since he hath ordered this
We have nought to do but still
Rest in silence on his will.

Also John Short, husband of the above / Reunited Aug 13, 1954

At rest

14. *(flat and overgrown, not all readable)*

In loving memory / of / my beloved husband / Morgan Jones /
who met his death in the Senghenydd / explosion Oct 14th 1913
aged 32 years.
Also .....

15. *(unusually, in the form of a cross; compare the verse in 3 and
22)*

In loving memory of / James / the beloved husband of / Sarah
Bevan / who lost his life in the / Senghenydd Colliery explosion
/ Oct 14th 1913, aged 32 years.

A sudden change at God's command he fell
He had no chance to bid his friends farewell
Affliction came without warning given
And did him haste to meet his God in heaven.

16. *(note: the baby died in September, and then the father in the
explosion)*

In loving memory of / Gomer / the beloved husband of /
Gertrude Green / Senghenydd / who lost his life in the /
Senghenydd Colliery explosion / Oct 14th 1913, aged 28 years

Also of their son / Albert / Died Sept 18, 1913, aged 7 months

17. In / loving memolry / of / Jeffrey J Davies / the beloved husband of / Mabel Davies / 31 Stanley St, Senghenydd / who met his death at the Senghenydd / Mine disaster Oct 14, 1913 / aged 27 years

Thy purpose Lord we cannot see / But all is well that's done by thee.

Also Mabel the above / who died Jan 13, 1920 / aged 35 years / RIP / Rest in the Lord

18. *(two brothers; beautiful stone)*

In / loving memory / of / Thomas Fern, (Aged 21) / Also / Richard M. Fern, (Aged 19) / 44 Francis St, Abertridwr / who lost their lives Oct 14th 1913 / at the Senghenydd explosion

They are gone, but not forgotten,
Never shall their memory fade;
Sweetest thought shall ever linger
Round the graves where they are laid.

19. In loving memory of / John / the beloved husband of / Helen Maude Mogridge / Abertridwr / who lost his life at the / Senghenydd Pithead, Oct 14th 1913 / aged 29 years.

"Therefore be ye also ready"

Also of the above / Helen Maude Mogridge / who died Dec 24th 1968 / aged 78 years

"At rest with the Lord."

20. *(died in the explosion - ?)*

Er cof am / Thomas David Jones / yr hwn a fu farw Hyd 14eg 1913 / yn 19 mlwydd oed.

Hefyd am fam yr uchod Jane Jones / yr hon a fu farw Gorph. 10fed 1929 / yn 68 mlwydd oed.

"Hyd doriad gwawr."

21. *(beautiful stone)*

Er / cof anwyl / am / Thomas Lewis / anwyl briod Mary Lewis / 95 Commercial Street, Senghenydd / Bu farw yn Nhanchwa Senghenydd / Hydref 14, 1913 / yn 62 mlwydd oed.

Hefyd Mary / gweddw anwyl yr uchod / Bu farw Awst 1, 1923 / yn 76 ml. oed

22. *(compoare with the verse in 3 and 15)*

In loving memory of / George Henry / the beloved husband of / Margaret Ann Evans / Senghenydd / who met his death at the / Universal Colliery / Oct 14th 1913, aged 25 years

A sudden change at God's command he fell,
He had no chance to bid his friends farewell,
Affliction came, without warning given,
And bid him haste to meet his God in heaven.

23. *(father and son)*

In loving memory of / Frederick / the beloved husband of / Mary Ann Williams / Senghenydd / who met his death at the / Universal Colliery Oct 14th 1913 / aged 42 years

Also of John, their beloved son / who met his death at the same / disaster, aged 18 years

"Be ye also ready"

Also of Mary Ann his wife / who died April 23 – 1941 / aged 70 years

24. *(three brothers, from Blaenau Ffestiniog; beautiful stone)*

Er cof anwyl am / Richard Evans, / 25 mlwydd oed. / William Evans, / 22 mlwydd oed. / Robert Evans, / 19 mlwydd oed. / Tri o feibion John a Jane Evans, / Dolgaregddu, Bl. Festiniog / fuont feirw yn Nhanchwa Alaethus Senghenydd / Hydref 14, 1913

25. *(beautiful stone; the couplet is in cynghanedd)*

Er coffadwriaeth am / Richard / anwyl briod Margaret Kirkham / 67 High St, Senghenydd / a fu farw Tachwedd 14, 1913 / yn 63 ml. oed

"Am hynny byddwch chwithau barod"

Hefyd am John Richard / anwyl fab / John Richard a Margaret Kirkham / a gollodd ei fywyd yn / Nhamchwa Senghenydd, Hydref 14, 1913 / yn 20 ml oed.

"O'r lofa trwy Ddamchwa ddwys,
Ehedodd i baradwys."

Hefyd Margaret Mary / anwyl briod Thomas Walters / 107 High St, Abertridwr / yr hon a fu farw ar y 4ydd o Ionawr 1918 / yn 43 mlwydd oed.

"Gwerthfawr yn ngolwg yr Arglwydd / yw marwolaeth ei saint ef."

Gwenllian Aubrey

The legacy

Community, Memory and History:
Senghenydd and the Valleys
Neil Evans

The setting of the south Wales coalfield in a series of deeply incised valleys is one of its most distinctive features. The term 'the valleys' emerged in the course of the nineteenth century as the population moved down from the blaenau; it displaced the older references to 'the hills'. Attention shifted away from the physical environment and towards the new population of the area. The 'hills' were an alien and hostile world: the 'valleys' were a container for a community. The idea has become a vital component of Welsh identity despite the continuing slippage of the population towards the valley mouths and the coastal strip. Within Wales it locates people effectively in a common experience and sometimes in opposition to other Welsh experiences, even if this is muddied by the indiscriminate use of the term to describe the whole of Wales by outsiders.

Mining communities are frequently seen as being apart from the rest of society – perhaps most infamously in the headline which appeared in a Kent newspaper: 'Miner in Fight with Man'! In the 1950s there was even a sociological theory evolved by two Americans, Clark Kerr and Abraham Siegel, which purported to explain the militancy of miners in this way; they were an 'isolated mass'. In south Wales the geography compounds this sense of isolation. This is particularly true in the tiny Aber Valley, an offshoot of the Rhymney Valley, which was opened up for exploitation in the 1890s in the final heave of the coalfield's growth. A decade earlier it had narrowly escaped the fate of being flooded to provide water for Cardiff which is only a dozen miles away in physical distance though much further in any other terms. In the 1890s two coalmining communities and two pits: Abertridwr and Senghenydd; Windsor and Universal – were created here. The second of them is the subject of Michael Lieven's book, *Senghennydd: The Universal Pit Village, 1890-1930* (Gomer Press, 1994).

I always look at Senghenydd in two ways. The oldest and the simplest is just that it is where I grew up and it has the kind of associations which mark childhood and adolescence. Yet to grow up there in the 1950s was to be aware of the wider significance of the place. It is one of the most famous villages in Wales, with a resonance far beyond that it has for its natives. Just as Treddol will be associated with the 1859 revival and Blaenannerch with that of 1904–05, Senghenydd means blood on the coal. In my childhood it often seemed to be locked into the events of 14 October 1913 when 439 miners died in an explosion. Lieven provides a particularly graphic account of the explosion.

My grandfather had left mid-Wales in the 1890s and could remember Senghenydd Square when it was simply a farm. The remains of the pit brooded over the village as a reminder of destruction. There were still living survivors; the men who had been ill, drunk or rescued, and there seemed always to be television crews seeking them out. Suddenly the old men who passed their declining days clustered around the war memorial became national and local celebrities. It was still a mining community despite the closure of Universal in 1928; my father drove buses and took miners to Bedwas, Penallta and Nantgarw. Many others walked to Windsor in Abertridwr, returning with the characteristic blocks under their arms.

As I was making that discovery others were taking the first steps to produce a formal history of the community. As the earliest migrants were dying out in the 1950s the YMCA did a pioneering oral history project to record their memories. A local headmaster, Basil Phillips, began to investigate archives, while Barry Owen, the barber, was amassing old photographs though his work was eventually eclipsed by Bill Styles, a quite extraordinary collector. By the 1970s these ventures were beginning to bear fruit; Basil Phillips wrote some pioneering articles in the local history journal *Caerphilly* and promised a full-scale history. In the 1980s local investigation took off. It paralleled exactly the demise of the industry locally: Windsor closed in 1977, and within a few years a memorial has been erected to the victims of 1913. The Senghenydd Community

Council continued this work by establishing a Book of Remembrance set in a room which traces the history of the community in general and the disaster in particular. Memorial services have been held and a facsimile edition of the *Book of Remembrance, Universal Colliery, Senghenydd, 1901: 1913* (ed. J. Basil Phillips and David G. Parry) made available for sale.

Books began to tumble from the presses. John Brown wrote a serious and substantial history one, *The Valley of the Shadow: An Account of Britain's Worst Mining Disaster: The Senghenydd Explosion* (Alun Books, Port Talbot, 1981). William Boulton's *Senghenydd: The Village and its Rugby Club* (Starling Press, Risca, 1982) put a a far less disastrous enterprise at the centre of affairs while Elias Evans wrote his anecdotal *The Aber Valley: The Story of a Mining Community* (Village Publishing, Risca, 1987). It included a list of nicknames of local characters which gives something of its flavour. I have never been able to forgive him fully for leaving out 'Bill Cop 'orse' (the former roundsman of the Ynysybwl Co-operative Society, for foreigners), a much-loved character from my youth. Basil Phillips has finally produced the first volume in what he promises will be three on the history of the valley: *Abertridwr Through the Ages* (Starling Press, Rogerstone, 1991). It is meticulously researched and clearly a labour of love. Proving that the personal is political Richard Felstead wrote *No Other Way: Jack Russia and the Spanish Civil War* (Alun Books, Port Talbot, 1984) a biography of his grandfather, Jack Roberts. Howard C. Jones edited *Old Caerphilly and District in Photographs* (Stewart Williams, Barry, 1979) which enabled us to see the entire industrial history of the valley through the lenses of visiting photographers.

Mike Lieven's book is full of shopkeepers and social elites, something which might disturb some of the more romantic notions of classless solidarity. Certainly Senghenydd had no developed elite and most felt the pressures of the turbulent history. This was especially true in the great strikes of the 1920s when shopkeepers often teetered on the edge of bankruptcy after extending credit to strikers. Any realistic account of the valleys will have to confront the kind of social divisions which did exist. In my day there was still an elite; compared with the current dereliction there was a veritable shopping centre in the 1950s and 60s and the shopkeepers were the leading figures. They had their own room in the local club; never totally exclusive, of course, but dominated by them. Deacons were sometimes drawn from them but generally they were a fairly secular lot, amongst the foremost local beneficiaries of the affluence of the Macmillan years. The deacons I remember often worked in the pit, though usually not as coalface workers. Nor did councillors did not spring from the shopocracy. It was said that you could map the priorities in council's tarring of backlanes in the 60s by noting where the councillors lived.

Other divisions were superimposed. There were many houses owned by the NCB and they had a lower social cachet than the privately owned remainder. There was some association between these housing classes and the streaming in the schools. If you were one of the select few who passed the eleven plus it provided another division, physical in the daily journey to Caerphilly and social. One boy never spoke to me after I passed the exam. Yet this marked a more important class boundary; anyone coming from the valleys was crossing a divide. The official school history is nostalgic for the days when there were mainly middle class boys from the town to educate. People like me made the school materialistic, it was alleged. Fewer girls than boys made the journey. Another division by the 1950s was between working in the coal industry and not; I referred to 'the park'. My friend whose father was an overman to 'the welfare'. This language symbolised different worlds of experience; not all had the sense of community reinforced by the world of work, however vicariously. And there were the divisions of gender; the Ex-¬Servicemen's Club still refuses to admit women to any category of membership. This is quaintly justified in terms of artisan respectability: wives can allow their husbands to drink safe in the knowledge that they are not cavorting sexually. The club imposes its own standards: strict bans on swearing and the risk of going before the committee.

What the book raises in a broader way is the whole identity of the valleys. The efforts to write local history in the area have been going on for a couple of decades at least and are generally a broader reflection of the process I have described in more detail for Senghenydd. The old intimate connection with the past has been severed and a new link needs to be established. In some places, I am told, young people lack any sense of the history of their valley communities. Local historians have been supplying the need to people who often, it seems, lack any organic connection to their past. It is no surprise that a central character in Christopher Meredith's brilliant novel Shifts is a local historian or that he is being displaced from a steelworks. In that he symbolises the experience of a generation. Much of the modern identity of Wales rests on images of this industrial area and it has suffered hammer blows in the 1980s. Recovery of the past is one way of coping. This involves a wider trawl than the industrial history of the area; for some, at least, in includes a sense of the loss of the Welsh language and an effort to restore it.

The process of creating a history for the valleys is a much older one though it has always been beset with difficulties. There were attempts to do it in the nineteenth century; Moses Williams wrote eisteddfod essays on the history of the Rhondda around the turn of the century and 'Morien' produced his *History of Pontypridd and the Rhondda Valleys* in 1903. They share a failure to find a way to organise their material. Williams provided salvoes of statistics which demonstrate growth and then became totally anecdotal and episodic. Morien took this tendency to its extreme; his book has a chapter on the writing of the Marseilles within it! What was lacking was any real notion of social history and consequently of the way in which the history of a community could be written. Not all were hindered by this as the various Powells produced a notable History of Tredegar in 1882 (revised and extended 1902) but it does seem to have been a general problem. Many of the writers were in any case trying to recreate the lost pre-industrial world of their communities which was just slipping out of reach. Williams had a Proustian sense of loss about the fairy circles of the Rhondda! Their modern equivalents, by contrast, are trying to reclaim the now vanishing industrial past. The late nineteenth century effort to understand was elaborated in a host of journalistic pieces on the intrusion of industry into the beautiful wilderness of Wales. *How Green was My Valley* and ultimately *The Rape of the Fair Country* issued effortlessly out of this. The valleys acquired the image by which the world came to know them.

Historians have done something to rescue the valleys from this morass in the meantime but this has not fully connected with local and lived experience. Hence the proliferation of local histories and autobiographies which speak to these needs. What is necessary is something beyond local history: the danger is that the proliferation of local studies will leave us with simply local consciousness floating freely in an undifferentiated international culture. Lieven points us towards community studies which connect with the coalfield, Wales, the UK, Europe and beyond. His book appeared in the year that British Coal shut its last deep mine in south Wales. As that era ends the challege is to reinterpret the past as well as to develop a new future. 'The hills' became 'the valleys' in the last century: what will the valleys become in the next? They deserve a future more vital than as an impoverished ghetto adjacent to the M4 corridor, those parts of the past not yet forced into the increasingly well-filled mouths of the valleys and the ports which owe their modern existence to what once went on in the hills.

Senghennydd

(439 lost their lives in a pit disaster,
October 14, 1913)

Their names shall lose meaning,
features forgotten,
as surely as the years
erase the tide's story
leaving no trace.

And yet, after the savage coal-face
claimed arms and limbs,
their deaths have left a void
as vivid as the sky's emptiness
when a star falls;
a grief as solid as their gravestones,
as tender as our tears.

Rhydwen Williams

*Memorial 1981: it is hoped that a new memorial
will be erected by public subscription*

Glossary

Sliding Scale The system where the workmen's wages was fixed by the selling price of coal. It was brought into being in 1875 and stopped with the conciliation agreement of 1905. It was heavily biased against the workmen.

Trams Also called drams, tubs or latterly mine-cars. A sort of mini railway wagon used to convey coal out of the mine, and supplies into the mine. They could vary in the weight carried, from one to two tons.

Journey A number of trams linked together and attached to a steel rope and brought out of the mine by a haulage engine. Normally a journey would consist of twenty-four to twenty-eight trams.

Overman The man in charge of a particular area of the mine: it could vary from a coalface to the whole of the underground workings in the absence of the manager or under-manager.

Bank/ Banksman The top of the pit/the man who controls the shaft operations from the surface. That is the raising and lowering of men and materials.

Afterdamp Also called blackdamp. It is the atmosphere left in a mine following an explosion of gases. The oxygen in the air has been used in the explosive mixture leaving a cocktail of deadly gases, mainly carbon monoxide, which can prove fatal.

Firedamp Also called methane. It is a gas accumulated in pockets in coal seams and given off when the coal is disturbed. It can cause an explosion when it consists of between 5 and 16 per cent of the air in a mine and comes into contact with a flame or spark.

Hitcher The man who controls the winding operations at the bottom of the shaft. That is, the raising and lowering of men and materials.

Laggings	Timber placed behind steel arches to prevent debris falling through.
Fireman	The early name for a deputy. The name was derived from his duty of detecting gas and 'firing' small amounts so as to make the workplace safe for the men to enter. A deputy is responsible for all safety issues within a working area.
A jump	A geological fault within a coal seam where the coal 'jumps' up or down from its original level.
'Stopped'	A 'stopping' is a barrier to prevent workmen from entering dangerous old workings once a coalface has reached the end of its productive life.

References and Further Reading

John H. Brown, *The Valley of the Shadow* (Alun Books, Port Talbot, 2009)

J. Basil Phillips, *Senghenydd: a brave community* (Old Bakehouse Publications, Abertillery, 2002)

Ray Lawrence, *The Widows Wail: the Universal Colliery, Senghenydd, Explosions of 1901 and 1913* (1912)

Michael Lieven, *Senghennydd: The Universal Pit Village 1890–1932* (Gomer, 1994)

Mike Lieven, 'Representations of the Working Class Community: the Senghenydd Mining Disaster, 1913' in *Llafur*, vol. 5, no. 2, 17 ff

Neil Evans, 'Community, Memory and History' in *Planet*, No. 115, Feb–March 1996, pp. 47–55

Luther Thomas, *The Deep of the Earth* (Macmillan, 1956)

Walter Haydn Davies, *Ups and Downs* (Christopher Davies, Abertawe, 1974)

Acknowledgements

My thanks to those who helped with the compiling of this book, which I hope will be a fitting tribute to those who died in 1901 and 1913, and their families. From my conversations with family members it is clear that the disasters still hurt, and that there is still anger about the men's working conditions, and the way the pit management and the enquiries dealt with the disasters.

The paltry £24 fine for the pit owners and management in 1914 remains a massive scar on Welsh history.

I thank particularly Ceri Thompson, the curator of Big Pit, for his encouragement and for supplying photographs and captions.

Ray Lawrence's contribution to the book is invaluable – historical pieces on the Senghenydd disasters, the rescuers and glossary. Ray was born in Cwmcarn, and was the third generation of miners in his family. During his years at Celynen South Colliery at Abercarn he was Lodge Secretary of the National Union of Mineworkers for fourteen years, and was on the South Wales Area Executive Council of the NUM for three years. He took an active part in the 1984/5 miners' strike. Ray later became a probation officer, but since retirement has written many books on the mining industry in the south Wales coalfield. When in his 60s he earned his BSc from part-time study with the Open University.